CW00945490

Happy Cooking!

Les Abats

Les Abats
Michel Roux Jr

Recipes celebrating
the whole beast

SEVEN DIALS

This edition published in 2017 by Seven Dials,
an imprint of the Orion Publishing Group Ltd
Carmelite House
50 Victoria Embankment
London EC4Y 0DZ
An Hachette UK Company

10 9 8 7 6 5 4 3 2 1

Text copyright © Michel Roux Jr 2017
Design and layout copyright © Seven Dials 2017

The moral right of Michel Roux Jr to be identified as the author of this work has been
asserted in accordance with the Copyright, Designs and Patents Acts of 1988.

All rights reserved. No part of this publication may be reproduced, stored in a
retrieval system, or transmitted, in any form or by any means, electronic, mechanical,
photocopying, recording or otherwise, without the prior permission of both the
copyright owner and the above publisher.

A CIP catalogue record for this book is available from the
British Library.

ISBN: 978 1 4091 6895 9

Editor: Jinny Johnson
Designer: Lucie Stericker
Illustrator: Clairice Gifford
Proofreader: Elise See Tai
Indexer: Vicki Robinson
Photograph on page 8: Issy Croker

Printed and bound in Italy

www.orionbooks.co.uk

The Joy of Offal

Around 12.30pm one day in December 1999, four rather dilapidated middle-aged men and one handsome not-quite-middle-aged woman tripped up the steps into Le Gavroche and then downstairs to the dining room. Some four or so hours later four men and one woman marched out completely transformed, their faces so radiant with delight and pleasure that they lit up the gloom and chill of the winter afternoon. The four men were myself and my brothers, James, Johnny and Tom, and the woman was our sister, Elizabeth, and we had been feasting on delectable course after delectable course of offal. Each year since we have repeated the celebration.

Le Gavroche has always been a temple of delight and a home of civilised values. In my view nothing exemplifies its dedication to the higher levels of gastronomic beauty than the capacity of Michel Roux and his team to transform what many people feel are the base culinary metals of hearts, livers, kidneys, sweetbreads, brains, tripe and all the rest into the most exquisite and sensual of dishes.

How can I forget the operatic splendour of Tête de Veau à la Tortue à la façon Fernand Point, complete with succulent cockscombs and testicles; suckling pig stuffed with its own offal, the skin as thin and friable as a rime of frost, the flesh beneath tender and tasteful; the rustic, rollicking Sanguette 'Papi Marcel'; the melting cloud of Cervelles de Veau Meunière with tiny explosions of Petits Câpres et Persil Frits; the Turban de Veau à la Financière? How can I not smile at the memory of all the tripe, livers, kidneys, trotters, ears, intestines, testicles and tongues of calves, pigs, sheep, ducks and chickens that have provided such delicious accompaniments to our affectionate annual family gatherings?

Let's face it, offal is not a pretty word, but I would far rather have that blunt honesty than the verbal pussyfooting of the American 'variety meats', the Lebanese 'fifth quarter,' the Swedish 'innanmat' – interior food – or even 'the odd bits' as some would have us call them. Perhaps not surprisingly, the world is divided into those who recoil from the very thought of eating any interior organs, and those who sigh, 'Offal! How wonderful.'

I am of the latter class, passionately so. I've never been able to understand the aversion to offal. On a matter of principle, if you're going to raise animals to feed you, it seems responsible to eat as much of them as possible. On a matter of practicality, these meats are highly nutritious. Many are low in calories. They're easy to digest, and they're cheap – the perfect modern dietary food, in other words.

But, above all, offal is a source of gastronomic enchantment, for both cook and consumer. Each type of offal has its own character, a character that stand up to the most potent sauces and the punchiest of accompaniments. The flavours are subtle, distinctive and enduring, and the textures varied, fine grained and seductive. There is variety and verve in each one.

And I can think of no better source of inspiration than recipes from a chef whose own offal dishes have given me so much joy over the years.

As my mother used to murmur when I recounted the details of yet another Lucullan Fort family offal lunch: 'Oh, I DO love brains.'

Matthew Fort

Les abats, or offal, are the inside bits of an animal – the heart, liver, kidneys, brain, tongue, even lungs – as well as the extremities, such as the tail, ears and feet. For some, the idea of offal sets the mouth watering; others view it with alarm.

For centuries, it was taken for granted that you ate every part of an animal, that nothing should be thrown away. This is still the case in many parts of the world, but in the UK and US offal fell out of favour for a long while. But now things are changing – we're seeing crispy pig's ears on menus, butchers are selling hearts and marrow bones, and people are cooking offal again. We're realising that if we are to eat animals we should respect them, and that means not wasting any part. So-called 'nose to tail eating' is gaining popularity.

I grew up eating offal. My mother would often cook lamb's liver – but it was pink, sweet and delicious, not the leathery overcooked horror I experienced at school. Kidneys were a regular in our house and brains were a real treat. Whenever family members came to visit us from France they would bring parcels of boudin noir and andouillette.

When I worked with the great Alain Chapel at his restaurant in Mionnay he always had offal on the menu – I've included one of his recipes for sheep's trotters in this book. At Le Gavroche we've always featured offal and we're finding that people are becoming more adventurous and love to try unfamiliar dishes.

Offal is generally cheap and always nutritious. In this book I've included recipes for the parts I think are good to eat and that are of gastronomic value. There's everything from a quick and delicious pasta with chicken giblets to the more challenging stuffed pig's head. Offal is simply meat – there's nothing to be scared of – and I hope you will enjoy cooking and eating some of these splendid dishes.

LES

ABATS DE LA MER

LES ABATS DE LA MER: *the offal of the sea, the liver, roe, head and other parts of fish and shellfish.*

Fish and shellfish are not the first things you think of in connection with offal. In northern Europe and the US we have a tendency to eat mostly fish fillets. They're easy to cook, appeal to everyone – and they don't look too fishlike! Many people don't like to see a whole fish on their plates, with eyes and fins and tail reminding us of its life in the sea. But this means we waste so much – and miss out on some great tastes and textures.

Other cultures are more adventurous. In Japan and Sardinia they cure tuna hearts and eat fish ovaries and semen. In Portugal and parts of South America cod tripe is a popular dish. And in the Arctic Circle people eat plenty of fish liver, as it is an excellent source of vitamin D, the sunshine vitamin.

Watch a fishmonger filleting a fish for you and you will see more than half of it fall into the stock bucket, but much of this can be eaten and enjoyed. As with pigs, cattle and fowl, it's important to respect the whole animal and eat as much of a fish as we can. Fish heads, for instance, contain lots of flavour and goodness. They're useful in stocks but also make a great fish soup. The collar – the section behind the head – of fish such as salmon and tuna is very meaty and tasty. Collars are much enjoyed in Asia and far cheaper than fillets. Other parts of the head, such as cheeks and tongues or throats – the part under the fish's mouth – can also be made into superb dishes.

Fish eggs, or roe, can be smoked or dried and used in a variety of dishes, while fish liver is extremely rich and nutritious. Best of all fish livers is monkfish, which is superbly rich and nutritious.

So instead of buying cod fillet or salmon steaks, try asking your fishmonger for a couple of fish heads or some cod cheeks. Whizz up some cod roe and make your own taramasalata, and instead of throwing away scallop trimmings, fry them to make a crispy snack to serve with aioli. There's more to a fish than fillets.

Monkfish Liver and Cabbage Slaw

Monkfish liver is a real gourmet treat, with a beautiful texture and a wonderfully delicate flavour – some call it the fois gras of the sea! Like cod liver, it's very good for you too. It's not that easy to come by, but you can ask your fishmonger to order it and there are also suppliers online. Once the liver has been marinated and cooked as below, it keeps for up to a week in the fridge.

Serves 4

1	fresh monkfish liver
pinch	all-purpose curing salt
1 tbsp	chartreuse
	croutons (see page 253), to serve
	salt and freshly ground black pepper

Cabbage slaw

½	savoy cabbage, finely shredded
3	carrots, peeled and grated
2	red onions, peeled and finely sliced
300g	mayonnaise (see page 251)
¼	red cabbage, finely shredded

Rinse the liver under cold running water for 15–20 minutes. Drain and pat it dry, then remove the main bloodline with a small pointed knife. Lay the liver out on a tray and season it with salt, pepper and a pinch of curing salt, then sprinkle over the chartreuse. Cover the liver and leave it to marinate in the fridge for about 20 minutes.

Cut the liver into 3 pieces and lay each one on a sheet of cling film. Roll up each piece of liver to form a cylindrical shape and twist and tie the ends of the cling film.

Place the liver parcels in a steamer pan, or in a bamboo steamer or colander over a pan of simmering water, and steam them for 20 minutes. Remove the liver and leave it to cool completely, then put it in the fridge.

To make the slaw, mix the savoy cabbage, carrots, onions and mayonnaise in a large bowl and season well – don't add the red cabbage until the last minute so the colour doesn't bleed.

Remove the cling film from the liver. Cut the liver into discs of about 1.5cm thick. Be sure to leave them out of the fridge for a few minutes before serving.

Just before you're ready to eat, mix the red cabbage into the slaw and serve it with the monkfish liver and baguette croutons.

Cod Cheek and Roe Kedgeree

*This is a splendid variation on the usual smoked haddock
kedgeree. Cod cheeks are readily available in most fishmongers
and are usually cheaper than cod fillet; they're convenient too,
as they don't contain any bones. Your fishmonger should also
be able to get smoked cod's roe for you and there are plenty of
online suppliers.*

Serves 6

120g	butter
2 tbsp	vegetable oil
1	large onion, peeled and diced
4	bay leaves
2 tbsp	curry powder
1 tsp	turmeric
6	cardamom pods, crushed
375g	basmati rice
750ml	vegetable stock
12	cod cheeks
1	whole smoked cod roe, skin removed
6	hard-boiled eggs
2	green chillies, thinly sliced
5	spring onions, chopped
2 tbsp	roughly chopped fresh coriander
	salt and freshly ground black pepper

Melt a tablespoon of the butter with a tablespoon of the oil in a large pan. Add the onion and cook it gently until it's translucent – don't allow it to brown. Add the bay leaves, spices and a little salt and pepper and continue to cook for 2–3 minutes. Add the rice and stir well to coat it with all the flavours.

Pour in the stock and bring it to the boil. Turn the heat down, cover the pan with a tight-fitting lid and simmer for 12 minutes. Take the pan off the heat and set it aside with the lid on.

Heat a tablespoon of butter with the remaining oil in a frying pan. Season the cod cheeks, add them to the pan and fry them gently until golden on both sides and cooked through. Remove them from the pan and set them aside somewhere warm. Slice the roe and warm the slices in the pan you used for the cod cheeks.

Peel and chop the hard-boiled eggs and add them to the rice with the chillies, spring onions and coriander. Fluff up the rice with a fork and add the remaining butter. Serve the rice topped with the cod cheeks and slices of roe. Some kale on the side is nice.

Fish Head Chowder

If you like, you can serve the fish heads whole in this creamy chowder. Some people, though, will find the heads a bit fiddly so it's probably best to do the work and remove all the edible morsels.

Serves 4

2	good-sized cod heads
1 tbsp	butter
2	medium potatoes, peeled and diced
2	large onions, peeled and diced
1	leek, white part only, washed and chopped
1	green chilli, halved
125ml	pastis
200ml	crème fraiche
	juice of 1 lemon
1 bunch	dill, chopped
	salt

Remove the gills from the cod heads, scrape off any scales, then rinse the heads in cold water. Melt the butter in a large saucepan, add the potatoes, onions, leek and chilli and cook gently for 5 minutes. Add the fish heads and pastis, then pour in cold water to cover. Season with salt, bring to a simmer, then loosely cover the pan with a lid and leave the soup to cook for 20 minutes.

Remove the pan from the heat, leave the soup to cool slightly, then carefully remove the heads. Pick out all the meat, cartilage and fatty morsels and discard the bones. Add the meat and other bits and pieces to the soup with the crème fraiche and lemon juice, stir gently and add the chopped dill before serving.

Salmon Head and Tofu Soup

A fishmonger should be happy to give you a salmon head for next to nothing and it makes an excellent soup.

Serves 2–4

1	salmon head
1 tbsp	olive oil
4	garlic cloves, peeled and finely chopped
30g	fresh root ginger, finely sliced
2	star anise
10	Sichuan peppercorns, tied in a muslin bag
25ml	rice vinegar
150g	soft tofu, diced
3	spring onions, chopped
handful	chopped fresh coriander
	salt and freshly ground black pepper

Scrape the scales off the fish head and remove the gills, then cut the head in half and rinse it in cold water. Heat the oil in a frying pan, add the garlic and ginger and sauté them gently. Add the star anise and the peppercorns, then the pieces of salmon head. Continue to cook until the fish starts to take on some colour.

Add 750ml of water and the rice vinegar, then bring to a simmer. Skim any scum from the surface and continue to simmer gently, uncovered, for 30 minutes. Pass the soup through a sieve, then add the tofu and spring onions and simmer for a further 10 minutes. Remove the star anise and peppercorns and season to taste.

Serve the soup with or without the head and garnish each bowlful with chopped fresh coriander.

Fried Scallop Skirts with Aioli

If you buy scallops in their shells to clean yourself you will find the frilly 'skirt' or mantle around the meat. Remove this, discard the black bits (digestive tract and intestine) and set the skirts aside. Keep them in the freezer until you have enough to use for this recipe. The skirts are delicious deep-fried, but they need long, slow cooking first to make them tender.

Serves 4 as a snack

12	scallop skirts
1 sprig	thyme
2	bay leaves
	vegetable oil, for frying
3–4 tbsp	potato flour, for dusting
	salt

Aioli

2	egg yolks
1 tbsp	Dijon mustard
	juice of 1 lemon
4–6	garlic cloves, peeled and finely crushed
100ml	vegetable oil
100ml	olive oil
	salt and white pepper

Soak the skirts in cold water for a couple of hours, then rinse them under running cold water to remove any grit or sand. Place them in a pan with the thyme, bay leaves and a good pinch of salt, cover with cold water and bring to the boil. Skim off any scum, then turn the heat down to a very gentle simmer and cook the skirts for 2–3 hours or until tender. You may need to top the pan up with boiling water from time to time. Once the skirts are tender, drain, pat them dry and leave them to cool.

Half-fill a large saucepan or a deep-fat fryer with vegetable oil and heat to 180°C. Dust the skirts with potato flour and deep-fry them until crisp, then season with salt before serving with the aioli.

To make the aioli, whisk the eggs yolks in a bowl with the mustard, lemon juice and garlic and season with salt and pepper. Slowly whisk in the oils until the mixture has emulsified.

Or if you prefer, blitz the egg yolks, mustard, lemon juice, garlic and seasoning in a blender. Slowly add the oil while the blender is running until the mixture has emulsified.

Salt Cod Tripe with Chickpeas and Smoked Paprika

Cod tripe is a real treat if you can manage to find it. It has a dense texture similar to squid, but it's a little more gelatinous and is usually sold salted.

Serves 6 as a starter

400g	salt cod tripe
1	celery stick
1 sprig	thyme
2	bay leaves
80g	dried chickpeas
4	shallots, peeled
12	garlic cloves, peeled
8	plum tomatoes
2 tbsp	olive oil
1 tbsp	smoked paprika
200ml	dry white wine
pinch	dried chilli flakes
	salt

Deep-fried parsley

1 bunch	flatleaf parsley
	vegetable oil, for frying

Soak the tripe in plenty of cold water overnight, then rinse it well. Remove any black skin and cut the tripe into medium-sized strips.

Place the tripe in a large saucepan with the celery, thyme and bay leaves. Cover generously with water, bring to a simmer, then cook for 90 minutes or until tender. Take the pan off the heat and leave the tripe to cool in the liquid.

Meanwhile, soak the chickpeas for an hour in warm water, then rinse them and put them in a saucepan with 1 whole shallot. Add water to cover, then simmer the chickpeas for 90 minutes or until fully cooked. Take the pan off the heat and leave the chickpeas to cool in the liquid.

Blanch the garlic cloves in salted, boiling water, then drain and repeat. Set them aside. Blanch the tomatoes in boiling water for a few seconds, then refresh them in iced water. Peel the tomatoes, deseed them and roughly chop the flesh.

Slice the remaining shallots. Heat the olive oil in a large pan, add the shallots and sweat them until translucent. Add the tomatoes, drained chickpeas and paprika and simmer for 3–4 minutes, then add the wine and garlic and simmer for another 3–4 minutes.

Finally, add the tripe with a little of the cooking liquid and simmer for 20 minutes. Season with salt and chilli flakes to taste and serve in bowls garnished with crispy deep-fried parsley.

For the parsley, wash it well, then make sure it is really dry. Half-fill a saucepan or a deep-fat fryer with vegetable oil and heat it to 180°C. Drop in some of the parsley – not too much at a time, as it will spit – and fry it for 20 seconds, then remove and drain on kitchen paper. Repeat to fry the rest.

Cod Tongues with Spiced Red Cabbage

The cod 'tongue' is not actually a tongue but a bit of muscle from the fish's throat and is well worth cooking for its taste and moist, succulent texture. You won't see them in fishmongers, but ask if they can get some for you – they're often thrown away.

Serves 4 as a starter or snack

3 tbsp	olive oil
3	shallots, peeled and finely chopped
2	garlic cloves, peeled and finely chopped
½	red chilli, chopped
½	red cabbage, finely sliced
100ml	cider vinegar
	flour, for dusting
12	cod tongues
	salt and freshly ground black pepper

Heat a tablespoon of the oil in a large saucepan, add the chopped shallots and cook them gently for 4–5 minutes. Add the garlic and chilli and cook for a further 4 minutes.

Add the sliced red cabbage and sauté everything together for 8–10 minutes until the cabbage is tender but still has some bite. Add the vinegar and cook for another 5–6 minutes over a low heat.

Spread the flour on a plate and season it with salt and pepper. Dust the cod tongues with flour. Heat a frying pan with the remaining olive oil and fry the cheeks on both sides until golden brown. Do this in batches if you need to, adding more oil if necessary. Serve the tongues on a bed of spiced red cabbage.

Cod Tongues and Cheeks

Cod cheeks are just that – and they are lovely little boneless morsels that are delicious fried. They are great combined with the cod 'tongues', but if you can't get tongues, you can make this recipe with cheeks only.

Serves 4

	flour, for dusting
700g	cod tongues and cheeks
	olive oil
	salt and freshly ground black pepper

Put the flour on a plate and season it with salt and pepper. Dust the tongues and cheeks all over with seasoned flour and set them aside.

Heat a heavy frying pan and add enough olive oil to cover the base of the pan. Add the tongues and cheeks, then fry them for a few minutes on both sides until golden brown and cooked through. You may need to do this in batches so you don't overcrowd the pan.

Drain the cod on kitchen paper and season with salt, then serve with tartare sauce (see page 254) and a crisp green salad.

Hake Throats 'Al Pil Pil'

Hake throats are a great delicacy in the Basque region of Spain and this is one of the classic ways of cooking them. This dish is all about texture – the throats are gelatinous and salty. The throats aren't easy to find outside of Spain, but ask your fishmongers if they can order some for you.

Serves 4 as a starter

350ml	mild olive oil
1	garlic clove, peeled and finely sliced
700g	hake throats
	squeeze of lemon juice
4	thin slices of red chilli
	salt

You need a large shallow pan that's wide enough to hold all the throats in a single layer. Add the oil and garlic to the pan and place it over a gentle heat. When the garlic starts to move about in the oil, gently add the throats to the pan. Keep the pan over a low heat and cook for them for 5-6 minutes.

Take the pan off the heat, gently remove the throats from the pan and set them aside to keep warm. Carefully drain off the oil from the pan and reserve it.

Place the pan back over the heat and add 3 tablespoons of water and a squeeze of lemon juice. Slowly start adding the oil back into the pan a little at a time, constantly shaking or twirling the pan to incorporate the oil and water. Continue until the mixture has emulsified. Add the chilli and season with salt, then pour the sauce over the throats and serve, perhaps with some crusty bread.

Teriyaki Salmon Collars

The collar is the part of the fish just behind the head and gills and includes the pectoral fins. All fish have collars but those of salmon and tuna are particularly tasty and much cheaper than fillet. Collars are very popular in Japanese cuisine but they are often thrown away in the UK. They come with the skin on and it should not be removed.

Serves 2

2 tbsp	sake
2 tbsp	mirin
3 tbsp	brown sugar
400ml	soy sauce
20g	fresh root ginger
1	green or red chilli, chopped
	grated zest of 1 lime
4	salmon collars
	olive oil
	lime wedges, to serve

To make the marinade, place the sake and mirin in a small saucepan and bring them to the boil to burn off the alcohol. Put the brown sugar and soy in another pan and heat gently until the sugar has dissolved. Add the sake and mirin and bring the mixture back to the boil. Remove the pan from the heat, add the ginger, chilli and lime zest and leave the marinade to cool.

Once the marinade is cold, place the salmon collars in a dish and pour the marinade over them. Leave for 4–6 hours in the fridge.

When you're ready to cook, heat a griddle or a barbecue. Remove the collars from the marinade, brush them with a little olive oil and place them on the hot griddle, skin-side down. Cook them for about 5 minutes on each side, brushing them with the marinade from time to time. Serve with lime wedges.

Taramasalata

*This popular dip is very easy to make for yourself at home.
It won't be pink like the supermarket versions, but if you want
some colour, just add a touch of beetroot juice.*

Makes 1 large bowlful

100g	white bread, crusts removed
	milk
250g	smoked cod's roe
	juice of 1 lemon
250ml	olive oil
	freshly ground black pepper

Place the bread in a bowl and add enough milk to cover. Leave the bread to soften, then drain off any excess milk.

If the roe is dry on the outside, peel off the thin skin. Put the roe in a food processor with the drained bread and pulse together until smooth. Add some of the lemon juice and season with pepper. With the processor running, add the olive oil until the mixture is well combined and has the texture you like – you might not need all the oil.

Taste for seasoning and add more pepper and lemon juice to taste. Serve with grilled bread or pitta and some crunchy lettuce.

Scallop Roe Taramasalata

Save and freeze the roes from any scallops you cook until you have enough to make this excellent variation on the regular taramasalata. If you don't have a stove-top smoker, you can use your barbecue or make your own smoker in an old pan with some foil and a steamer.

Makes 1 large bowlful

250g	scallop roes
100g	white bread, crusts removed
	milk
200ml	olive oil
50ml	lemon juice
	coarse sea salt and white pepper

Wash and dry the roes and sprinkle them liberally with coarse sea salt. Leave them for 20 minutes, then rinse off the salt and dry the roes. Bring a pan of salted water to the boil, add the roes and blanch them for 1 minute. Drain the roes and set them aside.

Heat a stove-top smoker with some wood chips. Add the drained scallop roes and smoke them for 20 minutes. Remove them and leave them on a plate, covered, to cool.

Cut the bread into cubes, put them in a bowl and add enough milk to cover. Leave the bread to soften, then drain and squeeze out any excess milk. Put the cooled roes in a food processor and add the bread. Blend, adding the oil in a steady stream. Season with salt, white pepper and the lemon juice to taste. Serve with grilled bread or pitta.

Roes on Toast

Milts or melts are the roes of male herrings, sometimes known as 'soft roes'. They were traditionally served as a breakfast dish or as a savoury but sadly seem to have gone out of fashion. They are a real delicacy and are rich in vitamin D, so this is a dish well worth reviving.

Serves 2

	plain flour, for dusting
8	herring roes or milts
1 tbsp	olive oil
	unsalted butter
2 slices	sourdough bread
	lemon juice
2 tbsp	chopped flatleaf parsley
	salt and freshly ground black pepper

Season the flour with salt and black pepper. Lightly dust the roes with the seasoned flour.

Heat the oil in a frying pan, add the roes and a knob of butter. Gently fry the roes for 5–6 minutes until they are golden brown all over. Meanwhile, toast the bread.

Remove the pan from the heat and add a splash of lemon juice and the chopped parsley. Butter the toast, spoon the roes on top and serve at once.

LA
VOLAILLE

LA VOLAILLE: *poultry*

Chicken livers are an easy entry into the world of offal. They're cheap, available, quick to cook – and delicious to eat. When buying livers, look for the lighter coloured ones – the darker the liver, the stronger the flavour, so choose blondish livers if possible. If the livers you buy do look dark, soak them in a little milk before using and this will remove some of the bitterness. Duck livers are slightly richer but can be used instead of chicken livers in any of the recipes that follow, as can turkey livers.

The rest of the chicken bits – known as giblets – are equally tasty and nothing to be scared of. Don't throw them away. They add lots of goodness to stews, gravy and stocks and you can make a wonderful giblet soup that's really wholesome and full of flavour.

Harder to find in this country but hugely popular in other parts of the world are parts of the chicken such as feet and gizzards. Admittedly there's not much to eat on a chicken foot but the taste and texture are great, and a pile of deep-fried crispy chicken feet make a much more interesting snack to serve with an aperitif than crisps or crackers. Gizzards do need long slow cooking but are good in a stew or confit and even the little cock's kidneys (actually testicles) are well worth trying.

In France, chickens are often sold whole, with the head and comb, and even roasted like that so the comb goes beautifully crispy. Otherwise you can usually find piles of combs in butchers' shops and they can be boiled until tender, then deep-fried.

And don't forget chicken skin! Yes, it is fatty but it's cheap and good to eat. Cooked until crispy, it adds loads of extra flavour and texture to a salad.

Chicken Liver Gratin

This makes a perfect starter for a special meal and you can prepare it in advance, then keep it in the fridge, all ready to finish off just before you're ready to serve. It's important to use fresh (not frozen) livers for the best texture.

Serves 4

400g	fresh chicken livers
1 tbsp	vegetable oil
2	shallots, chopped
2 tbsp	chopped flatleaf parsley
1 tbsp	butter
220ml	double cream
160g	cooked basmati rice (about 65g raw)
	grated zest of 1 lemon
3 tbsp	grated Gruyère cheese
2	egg yolks
3 tbsp	grated Parmesan cheese
	salt and freshly ground black pepper

Trim the livers of any sinew and green bits. Season them with salt and pepper.

Heat the oil in a frying pan. Add the livers and sear them over a high heat, then add the chopped shallots, parsley and butter. Cook briefly, then remove the pan from the heat while the livers are still slightly under cooked and moist. Divide the contents of the pan between 4 individual gratin dishes or tip everything into one big dish. Preheat the oven to 220°C/Fan 200°C/Gas 7 and heat up your grill.

Pour the cream into a small saucepan and bring it to the boil. Add the rice and the lemon zest and simmer for 4–5 minutes, then season. Take the saucepan off the heat and mix in the Gruyère and egg yolks. Pour the cream mixture on to the livers and sprinkle over the Parmesan.

Put the gratin in the hot oven for 5 minutes, then finish it under a grill until beautifully golden on top. Serve at once.

Chicken Liver Salad

I love this as a starter or a stand-alone dish. As in the last recipe,
it's vital to use fresh livers, not frozen ones, as the livers loose
texture once frozen.

Serves 4

200g	chicken skin
320g	fresh chicken livers
1 tbsp	vegetable oil
1	shallot, peeled and chopped
2	garlic cloves, peeled and chopped
1 tbsp	clear honey
1	red chilli, sliced
1 tbsp	Xérès (sherry) vinegar
3 tbsp	walnut oil
220g	**mixed salad leaves (including radicchio or curly endive)**
	salt and freshly ground black pepper

Preheat the oven to 180°C/Fan 160°C/Gas 4. Take the chicken skin and scrape off any feathers that remain and any excess fat on the underside. Lay the skin flat on a baking tray, sprinkle it with salt and cover it with a sheet of greaseproof paper and another baking tray. Place it in the oven for 30 minutes.

Remove the top tray and the paper. The skin should be crisp and golden, but if it's not, put it back in the oven for another 10 minutes without covering. Leave the skin to cool, then break it into bite-sized crisps.

Trim the livers of any sinew and green bits. Dry the livers well on kitchen paper, then season them with salt and pepper.

Heat the vegetable oil in a large frying pan until smoking hot. Sear the seasoned livers for 30 seconds, then add the shallot and garlic. Continue to cook for another 2–3 minutes until the livers are cooked but still pink inside. Tip the livers, shallot and garlic into a salad bowl.

Put the pan back on the heat and add the honey, chilli and vinegar. Simmer for 30 seconds and then pour everything over the livers. Add the walnut oil, salad leaves and crispy skin and toss well before serving.

Chicken Liver Parfait with Green Peppercorns

Everyone loves a chicken liver parfait and it's easy to make.
Use a terrine if you have one, otherwise a small loaf tin is fine.

Serves 10–12

75ml	veal stock
400g	chicken livers, soaked in milk for 24 hours
1	garlic clove, peeled and chopped
pinch	grated nutmeg
2	eggs
450ml	double cream
2 tbsp	brandy
1 tbsp	green peppercorns in brine, drained and lightly crushed
	salt and freshly ground white pepper

Bring the veal stock to the boil in a small saucepan and continue to cook until it's reduced to 25ml. Set the stock aside to cool.

Drain the livers and discard the milk – the soaking removes any bitterness. Put the livers in a food processor with the garlic and grated nutmeg and season with salt and freshly ground white pepper. Blitz until smooth, then add the eggs and blitz again for 1 minute. Add the cream, brandy and the cooled reduced stock, then pass the mixture through a fine sieve. Stir in the green peppercorns.

Preheat the oven to 180°C/Fan 160°C/Gas 4. Butter a terrine or a small loaf tin and line it with greaseproof paper. Pour the mixture into the terrine or tin and cover it with foil. Place it in a roasting tin, then add hot water to come halfway up the sides. Cook the parfait for about an hour, checking after 40 minutes and then again at 10-minute intervals. It should be firm to the touch.

Remove the parfait from the oven and leave it to cool in the roasting tin. Once it's cool, put the parfait in the fridge to chill overnight.

To serve, dip the tin in hot water and turn the parfait out on to a board. Carefully remove the greaseproof paper and slice the parfait. Serve it with red onion chutney (see page 250) and toasted country bread.

Chicken Liver and Red Wine Risotto with Grilled Radicchio

Chicken livers make an excellent risotto and this is a rich and filling main course. It looks pretty too, topped with the rosemary twigs and the slightly charred radicchio.

Serves 4

750ml	red wine
4	rosemary twigs
1 tbsp	caster sugar
200g	chicken livers
100g	butter
2	shallots, peeled and finely chopped
1	garlic clove, peeled and finely chopped
180g	arborio rice
300ml	hot chicken stock
3 tbsp	olive oil
2 heads	radicchio or similar bitter leaves
	salt and freshly ground black pepper

Pour the wine into a saucepan and add a few rosemary needles and the sugar. Bring the wine to the boil and keep boiling until it has reduced by two-thirds. Pour the wine through a sieve into a jug and set it aside.

Trim the livers and remove any green bits. Set aside 4 whole livers and chop the rest very finely.

Heat 20g of the butter in a saucepan and sweat the shallots and garlic until soft. Add the rice and continue to cook for 3–4 minutes. Pour over the sieved wine and simmer gently until it has all been absorbed, stirring to stop the rice catching on the bottom of the pan.

Gradually add the hot stock, a little at a time, and continue to cook and stir. The rice will take 18–20 minutes to cook to 'al dente' and the texture of the risotto should be quite loose and creamy.

Add the chopped livers and plenty of seasoning – the liver will cook in a matter of seconds. After 30 seconds, take the saucepan off the heat and stir in the remaining butter.

Heat a couple of tablespoons of oil in a frying pan, season the whole livers and fry them until cooked but still nice and pink inside. Thread them on to the rosemary twigs.

Cut the radicchio into quarters and season them with salt and pepper. Brush the radicchio with some olive oil and cook on a griddle pan until lightly charred. Serve the risotto topped with the skewers of whole livers and the radicchio.

Chicken Giblet Soup

The best way to gather the ingredients for this soup is to stash the necks, wings, livers and so on in the freezer each time you buy a chicken. The chicken oysters are those delicious little nuggets of dark meat that lie each side of the backbone. They're beautifully tender and often said to be the chef's treat!

Serves 6

3	chicken necks, skinned
3	chicken gizzards
6	chicken wings, including tips
6	chicken livers
6	chicken hearts
6	chicken oysters
3 tbsp	unsalted butter
	olive oil
1 tbsp	flour
1 litre	chicken stock
1	bouquet garni (thyme, bay leaf, parsley stalks, rosemary)
2	celery sticks, sliced
3 tbsp	cooked long-grain rice,
	salt and freshly ground black pepper

Cut each chicken neck into 3 pieces and the gizzards in half. Cut the tips off the wings and set them aside, then trim the remaining wings to resemble lollipops. To do this, cut the wings in half and push down the meat to reveal the bone. Remove and discard the extra small bone in one half of the wing. Trim the livers and hearts, removing any green bits from the livers. The oysters should be fine as they are.

Heat a tablespoon of the butter with a little drizzle of oil in a large saucepan and brown the necks, gizzards and wing tips. Sprinkle in the flour and stir well until brown, then pour in the stock and 500ml of water. Add the bouquet garni and seasoning, then simmer for an hour or until all the meat is tender. Pass the soup through a strainer and keep it warm.

Pick the meat off the necks and slice the gizzards. Heat a tablespoon of butter in a small pan and gently cook the sliced celery until tender, then set it aside. Add the rest of the butter and a tablespoon of oil to the pan and fry the livers, hearts, lollipops and oysters until golden. Season with salt and pepper and keep the meat warm.

Add the cooked rice and celery to the soup and warm it through. Serve the soup in deep bowls and divide the roughly chopped meat between them.

Cockscomb and Cock's Kidneys Ragout with Leeks

Cockscombs are delicious and if you enjoy the texture of trotters, you will love them. Cock's kidneys ('rognons' in French) are in fact testicles and you'll find them on the inside of the carcass – they are about the size of a pecan nut. They're fairly easy to find in France and most good butchers elsewhere should be able to procure them for you. This recipe is a great way to try them.

Serves 4

2	leeks
1 bunch	thyme
80g	butter
6	cockscombs
4	bay leaves
½	carrot, peeled
1	onion, peeled
12	cock's kidneys
2 tbsp	plain flour
1 tbsp	olive oil
1	shallot, peeled and chopped
2	garlic cloves, peeled and chopped
100g	wild mushrooms, trimmed and wiped
120ml	dry white wine
	zest and juice of 1 lemon
2 tbsp	chopped flatleaf parsley
	salt and freshly ground black pepper

Preheat the oven to 200°C/Fan 180°C/Gas 6. Trim and wash the leeks and place them on a large piece of foil. Season with salt and pepper, add a little thyme and a knob of the butter, then fold the foil over and seal into a secure parcel. Place the parcel on a baking sheet and cook in the preheated oven for 40 minutes.

Scrape off any loose skin and feathers off the cockscombs and rinse them under cold water. Place them in a pan of cold water and add salt, 2 bay leaves, a sprig of thyme and the carrot and onion. Bring the water to the boil, skim and then simmer the cockscombs for 2 hours until tender and easy to pierce with the tip of a knife. Leave the cockscombs to cool in the water, then drain and cut them into 2 or 3 pieces, depending on size. Keep the stock for later.

Soak the cock's kidneys in cold water for an hour. Drain, then put them in a pan, cover with cold water and season with salt, 2 bay leaves and a sprig of thyme. Bring the water to the boil, then turn down the heat to a very gentle simmer and cook for 20 minutes. Leave the cock's kidneys to cool, then drain and carefully peel off the membrane using the tip of a knife. Dust the kidneys with seasoned flour.

Heat the oil with a knob of butter in a frying pan and fry the kidneys until golden. Remove the kidneys from the pan and set them aside. Discard the fat from the pan.

Add a fresh knob of butter to the pan and sweat the shallot, garlic and mushrooms until tender. Add the kidneys and cockscombs, then the wine and simmer for 2 minutes. Add 200ml of the stock the cockscombs were cooked in and simmer for 5 minutes. Season with salt and pepper and add a drop of lemon juice, a little zest and the chopped parsley. Finish with the remaining butter to enrich and thicken the sauce.

Take the leeks out of the foil, split them in half lengthways and serve the hot ragout on top.

Cockscombs and Cock's Kidneys with Tarragon

Fresh tarragon has a lovely aniseedy flavour which works well with the richness of this dish. If you can't get tarragon mustard, just add a bit more fresh tarragon and use Dijon mustard. This is excellent served with tagliatelle.

Serves 4

200g	cockscombs
4	bay leaves
2 sprigs	thyme
½	carrot, peeled
1	onion, peeled
200g	cock's kidneys
1 tbsp	oil
3	shallots, peeled and finely chopped
200ml	chicken stock
200ml	double cream
1 tbsp	tarragon mustard
2 tbsp	chopped fresh tarragon leaves, chopped
	tagliatelle, to serve
	salt and freshly ground black pepper

Scrape off any loose skin and feathers off the cockscombs and rinse them under cold water. Place them in a pan of cold water and add salt, 2 bay leaves, a sprig of thyme and the carrot and onion. Bring the water to the boil, skim and then simmer the cockscombs for 2 hours until tender and easy to pierce with the tip of a knife. Leave the cockscombs to cool in the water, then drain and cut them into 2 or 3 pieces, depending on size.

Soak the cocks' kidneys in cold water for an hour. Drain, then put them in a pan, cover with cold water and season with salt, 2 bay leaves and a sprig of thyme. Bring the water to the boil, then turn the heat down to a very gentle simmer and cook for 20 minutes. Leave the cocks' kidneys to cool, then drain and carefully peel off the membrane using the tip of a knife.

Place a sauté pan over a medium heat and add the oil. Add the chopped shallots and cook them for 2–3 minutes, then add the chicken stock and bring it to the boil. Allow it to reduce slightly before adding the cream and the mustard. Season with salt and pepper.

Add the cock's kidneys and the combs and warm them through gently. Add the chopped fresh tarragon leaves just before serving with freshly cooked tagliatelle.

Puffed Chicken Feet with Sweet Mustard Dip

These are a bit like prawn crackers but much tastier and more interesting, and they make a great snack to serve with drinks. You can make a big batch of dried feet and keep them for a couple of weeks, then just deep-fry them to serve.

Makes 24

24	chicken feet
1 sprig	thyme
2	bay leaves
1	celery stick
1	garlic clove
1	green chilli
1 tbsp	sea salt
	vegetable oil, for deep-frying

Sweet mustard dip

2 tbsp	honey
2 tbsp	English mustard
4 tbsp	mayonnaise
2 tbsp	wholegrain mustard

Wash the feet under running cold water and scrub them with a small brush. Put them in a large saucepan with the herbs, celery, garlic, chilli and salt and cover with cold water. Bring the water to the boil, then turn the heat down and simmer the feet gently for 3 hours. By this time the meat and cartilage should be soft and coming off the bones.

Using a small pointed knife and a pair of tweezers, carefully remove the nails and the larger bones from the feet. The smaller bones and the cartilage will be soft enough to eat.

Put the feet on a non-stick baking tray or mat and leave them in the oven at the lowest possible temperature – about 60–70°C – until they have completely dried out. This should take about 4 hours. Once dried, the feet can be kept in an airtight container for a couple of weeks.

To serve, half-fill a deep saucepan with vegetable oil and heat it to 180°C. Add a batch of feet and deep-fry them for a minute or so until they puff up. Remove and drain the feet on kitchen paper, then season with sea salt.

Mix the ingredients for the mustard dip and serve it with the puffed feet.

Spicy Chicken Feet

Chicken feet are a hugely popular delicacy in most parts of Asia and there's no reason why the rest of us shouldn't enjoy them too. They are cheap to buy and are said to be very good for you as they are rich in collagen, so why not give them a try? Ask your butcher to get some for you or check online for suppliers.

Serves 4

1kg	chicken feet, nails removed	2 tbsp	oyster sauce
	sunflower oil	4 tbsp	Chinese fermented black beans, well rinsed
20g	fresh root ginger, finely chopped	1 tbsp	sugar
4	garlic cloves, finely chopped	750ml	chicken stock
1	red chilli, finely sliced	5	spring onions, finely chopped
3 tbsp	soy sauce		sesame seeds

Scrub the chicken feet well. Heat a high-sided saucepan with a good dash of sunflower oil and fry the feet until browned. Do this in batches so you don't overcrowd the pan. Remove each batch from the pan as they are browned and set them aside. Add the ginger, garlic and chilli to the hot pan and fry them together.

Put the feet back in the pan and add the soy sauce, oyster sauce, black beans, sugar and stock. Bring the stock to the boil, cover the pan with a lid and simmer for 2 hours. Remove the lid and continue to simmer for another 15 minutes to reduce the sauce a little.

When the feet are cooked they should be soft and chewy. Garnish them with the spring onions and a sprinkling of sesame seeds and serve with basmati rice.

Chicken Feet in XO Sauce

This is not an elegant dish, but it's very good. Just enjoy getting messy as you nibble at the deliciously sticky little bones. XO sauce is a wonderful seasoning based on dried seafood that I first came across when working in Hong Kong and have loved ever since.

Serves 4

16	chicken feet
4	star anise
1	cinnamon stick
1	dried chilli
1 bunch	fresh coriander
4 tbsp	XO sauce
1 tbsp	clear honey
	salt

Wash the feet and give them a good scrub, then trim off the nails. Place the feet in a saucepan with the star anise, cinnamon, chilli and half the coriander. Add cold water to cover and season with a little salt. Bring the water to the boil, then turn the heat down and simmer the feet for about 2 hours or until they're tender. Leave them to cool in the liquid, then drain them and put them in a bowl.

Blitz the XO sauce with the honey until smooth. Add this mixture to the feet and mix until all the feet are smothered in the sticky sauce. Preheat the oven to 220°C/Fan 200°C/Gas 7. Tip the feet on to a baking tray and cook them in the oven until they're golden and crisp. Chop the rest of the coriander and sprinkle it over the feet, then serve immediately.

Braised Duck Tongues

These meaty little morsels are full of flavour and are easy to prepare. The tongues do have a some cartilage running through the middle, which you can remove if you like, but I think the crunch just adds to the pleasure of the dish.

Serves 4

500g	duck tongues
2	garlic cloves, crushed
1	lemongrass stick, bruised
4	star anise
2 tbsp	dark soy sauce
200ml	dry sherry
2 tsp	chilli flakes or 1 dried chilli
2 tbsp	brown sugar
30g	fresh root ginger, sliced
500ml	chicken stock
	salt

Place the tongues in a bowl, cover them with cold water and season generously with salt. Set them aside for an hour, then drain and rinse.

Put the drained tongues in a saucepan with the garlic, lemongrass, star anise, soy sauce, sherry, chilli, sugar and sliced ginger. Add the stock and if it's not enough to cover the tongues, top it up with water. Bring to the boil, then turn the heat down to a simmer, cover the pan with a loose-fitting lid and cook for 1 hour and 15 minutes. Remove from the heat and leave the tongues to cool a little before serving with some steamed rice.

Glazed Duck Necks

Ask your butchers if they can order the necks for you. Alternatively, duck necks freeze well so if you like cooking duck, you could collect the necks in the freezer until you have enough for this dish. This is a feast with an Asian feel. Knives and forks are no use – you have to get messy and eat these like ribs!

Serves 6

6	large duck necks		**Glaze**	
750ml	chicken stock	5 tbsp	honey
30g	fresh root ginger	2 tbsp	sesame oil
1	lemongrass stick, bruised	6 tbsp	hoisin sauce
1	dried chilli	1	lime, zest and juice
	salt	2 tbsp	dark soy sauce

Place the duck necks in a large saucepan with the stock, ginger, lemongrass and chilli. Top up with enough water to cover and season with a good pinch of salt. Bring to a simmer and cook the necks gently for 1 hour. Remove the pan from the heat and set it aside for 15 minutes.

Mix all the ingredients for the glaze together in a bowl. After 15 minutes, remove the necks from the pan and place them in a container. Pour over the glaze and leave them to cool fully. Put them in the fridge overnight.

The next day, preheat the oven to 180°C/Fan 160°C/Gas 4. Place the necks and in an ovenproof dish with the glaze and put them in the oven to warm through. Once the necks are hot, preheat a grill and place the dish underneath. Baste the necks occasionally with the glaze until they become sticky. Serve with some stir-fried pak choi.

Tagliatelle with Chicken Giblets

Pasta and meaty chicken giblets make a cheap, wholesome and truly delicious supper. Dried tagliatelle is probably the best to use for this dish, as its firmer structure stands up better to the hearty sauce.

Serves 4

2 tbsp	olive oil
4	chicken necks, skinned
8	chicken wings
1	onion, peeled and chopped
3	garlic cloves, peeled and chopped
½ tbsp	tomato paste
100ml	red wine
500ml	chicken stock
12	chicken livers, trimmed and green bits removed
1 tbsp	butter
12	sage leaves
400g	egg tagliatelle
	salt and freshly ground black pepper

Heat a tablespoon of the oil in a large saucepan. Add the necks and wings and brown them, then add the chopped onion and garlic and continue to cook for a few minutes.

Add the tomato paste and red wine, then bring to the boil. Add the stock, season lightly and leave to simmer for 90 minutes. By this time the meat should be soft and tender and easy to pick off the bones.

Remove the chicken necks and wings. Put the pan back on the heat and reduce the remaining liquid to make a syrupy sauce. Pick all the meat off the bones and put it back in the sauce.

Cut each chicken liver into 2 or 3 pieces and season them with salt and pepper. Heat the remaining oil in a frying pan and fry the livers until coloured on the outside and still a little pink in the middle. Add them to the sauce, stir and leave to simmer. Add the butter to the frying pan and quickly fry a few sage leaves to garnish each serving.

Cook the pasta in salted water. Drain the pasta, then fold in the sauce and meat. Add the sage leaves and serve at once.

Gizzards, Snails and Grapes

Rich red wine, earthy meaty flavour and tangy juiciness – this is autumn on a plate and a true delight! You can buy ready-cooked snails, which work well, and you can also make the dish even easier by using confit gizzards instead of cooking them yourself.

Serves 4 as a starter

8	gizzards (chicken or duck)
1	bay leaf
1 sprig	thyme
2	garlic cloves, smashed
200ml	veal or beef stock
12	grapes, peeled and deseeded
2 tbsp	brandy
8	small onions, peeled
2 tbsp	vegetable oil
500ml	red wine
1 tbsp	caster sugar
2	shallots, peeled and sliced
2 tbsp	butter
12	cooked snails
2 tbsp	chopped flatleaf parsley
	salt and freshly ground black pepper

If the gizzards are whole, cut them in half and rinse them under running cold water to clean out any grit.

Place the gizzards in a saucepan with the bay leaf, thyme, garlic and stock, season with salt and pepper, then cover generously with water.

Bring to the boil, skim, then continue to simmer gently for 90 minutes or until the gizzards are tender. You may need to top up the pan with a little hot water now and then. Leave the gizzards to cool in the pan, then strain the cooking liquor and set it aside.

Steep the grapes in the brandy and set them aside.

Bring a pan of salted water to the boil and blanch the onions for 60 seconds. Drain and refresh them in iced water, then cut them in half. Heat a tablespoon of the oil in a non-stick frying pan and fry the onions, cut-side down, until browned. Remove the onions from the pan and set them aside.

Pour the wine into a saucepan, add the sugar and bring to the boil. Continue to boil until the wine is reduced by half, then set aside.

Heat another tablespoon of oil in the saucepan, add the sliced shallots and cook them until caramelised. Add the cooking liquor from the gizzards and the reduced wine and simmer until you have a syrupy sauce. Pass this through a sieve and then whisk in a tablespoon of butter.

Heat the remaining butter in a pan until brown. Add the snails and gizzards and reheat until lightly coloured. Warm the grapes too. Divide the gizzards, snails, onions and grapes between 4 little earthenware pots and add the sauce. Sprinkle with chopped parsley and serve.

Grilled Duck Hearts with Cherries and Almonds

Serve these tasty morsels with a few leaves as a starter to a barbecue meal or as a snack with drinks. If using wooden skewers, soak them in cold water for half an hour first so they don't burn.

Serves 4

20	whole almonds, skinned
20	cherries
12	fresh duck hearts
2 sprigs	thyme, chopped
	olive oil
	salt and freshly ground black pepper

Put the almonds in a pan of cold water, bring the water to the boil and simmer for 2–3 minutes. Drain the almonds and set them aside to cool. The blanching softens the nuts and makes it easier to thread them on to skewers.

Stone the cherries using a stoner gadget and fill each cherry with an almond.

Cut the duck hearts in half lengthways. Thread the pieces on to skewers, alternating them with almond-stuffed cherries. Sprinkle the skewers with chopped thyme and a drizzle of oil and season with salt and pepper.

Heat a griddle pan or a barbecue. Cook the skewers over a high heat – about 30 seconds on each side should be about right for pink meat. Serve at once.

Duck Hearts in Red Wine Sauce

Duck hearts are tender and tasty and are used here instead of beef in a bourguignon-style dish. If you can't source them at your butchers, check online for suppliers. You need a dry, firm salami such as a saucisson sec – the soft types are not suitable.

Serves 4

20	duck hearts	2	garlic cloves, peeled and crushed
12cm	piece of salami		
1 tbsp	vegetable oil	1 tbsp	plain flour
12	button onions, peeled	100ml	port
12	button mushrooms, trimmed	300ml	red wine
		600ml	duck stock (chicken will do)
2 tbsp	butter		
1 tsp	tomato paste		salt and black pepper

The duck hearts should be ready to cook, but check them over and trim them if necessary. Cut the salami into 20 cubes and push a cube into each heart. Heat the oil in a large casserole dish and brown the onions and mushrooms. Remove them and set aside. Add the hearts and butter and brown the hearts all over.

Add the tomato paste, garlic and flour and mix well, then pour in the port and wine. Scrape the bottom of the pan to release all the tasty caramelised bits. Simmer for 5 minutes, then add the stock and simmer for another 20 minutes. Return the onions and mushrooms to the casserole dish, season with salt and pepper, then cover with a cartouche of greaseproof paper. Simmer for a further 30 minutes. By this time, the hearts should be tender and soft to the touch. Skim the surface and serve with boiled or mashed potatoes.

Duck Gizzard, Heart and Egg Salad

Your butcher should be able to order duck gizzards and hearts for you, but you can also buy packs of frozen gizzards online. This makes a lovely light main dish with plenty of flavour and texture.

Serves 4

	coarse sea salt
8	duck gizzards
8	duck hearts
700g	duck fat
1 sprig	thyme
2	garlic cloves, peeled and smashed
1	baguette
1 tbsp	white wine vinegar
4	duck eggs
2	shallots, peeled and finely chopped
2 tbsp	red wine vinegar
4 tbsp	olive oil
	bitter leaves, such as dandelion
	black pepper

Sprinkle a layer of sea salt on a baking tray, add the gizzards and hearts and sprinkle a little more salt on top. Set them aside for 45 minutes, then brush off all the excess salt.

Preheat the oven to 170°C/Fan 150°C/Gas 3½. Reserve 2 tablespoons of the duck fat and heat the rest in a roasting tin. Add the thyme and garlic, then the gizzards and hearts. Place the tin in the oven and roast the gizzards and hearts for an hour until tender. Leave them to cool completely in the fat. When they're cold, remove them from the fat and set them aside. Remove the thyme and garlic and keep the fat for another time.

Cut the baguette into thin slices, spread them with some of the reserved duck fat and toast them in a preheated oven (180°C/Fan 160°C/Gas 4) until crisp. Set aside.

To poach the eggs, bring a pan of water to the boil and add the vinegar, which will help set the white part of the egg. Crack the eggs into separate bowls. Swirl the water with a spoon, gently add the eggs and poach for 5–6 minutes or until cooked but with soft yolks. Carefully remove them with a slotted spoon and drain on kitchen paper.

Heat the rest of the duck fat in a non-stick frying pan. Add the gizzards and hearts and brown them on all sides, then reduce the heat and add the chopped shallots. Cook for a minute and then remove the pan from the heat. Add the red wine vinegar and olive oil to form a dressing. Season with black pepper.

Place some salad leaves on each plate and add a poached duck egg in the centre. Spoon over the warm gizzards and hearts and the dressing. Finish with some crisp baguette croutons.

Chopped Liver

Simple and delicious, chopped liver is a classic of Jewish cuisine and is great as a snack or a starter, served with toasted rye bread or crackers and salad leaves. The dish is said to have originated in medieval Germany where it was made with goose livers.

Serves 8

180g	chicken skin (optional)
100g	duck or goose fat
500g	chicken livers
1	large onion, peeled and chopped
2 tbsp	Madeira
4	eggs, hard-boiled
2 tbsp	chopped flatleaf parsley
	salt and freshly ground black pepper

Preheat the oven to 200°C/Fan 180°C/Gas 6. Scrape the chicken skin, if using, to remove any feathers and excess fat. Lay it out flat on a baking tray, sprinkle a little salt over it, then place another tray on top. Roast the chicken skin in the oven for 20 minutes, then remove the top tray and continue to cook until the skin is crisp.

Heat 2 tablespoons of the fat in a large frying pan until smoking hot. Season the livers and fry them a few at a time until they are brown on both sides but still a little pink in the middle – 3–4 minutes should be about right. Place the livers in a colander to drain while you fry another batch. It is important not to overcrowd the pan or the livers will boil and not brown properly.

Once all the livers are browned, fry the onion in the same pan with the remaining fat until cooked and light golden in colour. Add the Madeira and then tip the contents of the pan into a food processor. Add the livers and pulse for a few seconds – the mixture should be coarsely chopped. Scoop it into a bowl, season well and refrigerate.

Serve the chopped liver garnished with the chopped hard-boiled eggs and parsley. If using the skin, crumble it over the top for extra crunch and flavour.

Duck Livers in Whisky Cream

A dish with really intense flavours, this is rich and delicious but still very quick and easy to prepare. Once the ingredients are cooked, you could also blitz them in a food processor and pile them into a dish to make a duck liver parfait.

Serves 4 as a starter or 2 as a main dish

400g	duck livers, trimmed
1 tbsp	vegetable oil
25g	butter
3	shallots, peeled and finely chopped
70ml	whisky
150ml	chicken stock
100ml	double cream
1 tbsp	chopped flatleaf parsley
	salt and freshly ground black pepper

Check the livers and remove any green bits. Season the livers on both sides. Put a frying pan over a high heat and add the oil. When the pan is hot, sauté the livers very quickly until they are golden brown on both sides but still pink in the middle. Remove the livers from the pan and set them aside somewhere warm.

Put the pan back over a medium heat, add the butter and shallots and cook them for 2–3 minutes. Add the whisky and reduce until almost all the liquid has evaporated. Add the stock and continue to cook until reduced by half.

Add the cream to the pan and reduce to a sauce consistency. Check the seasoning and add salt and pepper as needed. Put the livers back in the sauce and warm them through gently. Finish with chopped parsley and serve at once.

LE
GIBIER

LE GIBIER: *game*

The offal of feathered game, such as pheasant, pigeon and partridge, isn't that easy to obtain but is well worth cooking if you can find it. I love game so whenever I buy birds I freeze any hearts and livers until I have collected enough to cook with. If necessary, you can always boost whatever you have with some chicken livers and you'll still get the benefit of that wonderful gamey flavour.

Sadly much deer offal probably ends up in pet food, but I think venison liver is one of the finest of all livers. It's beautifully soft in texture and the taste isn't as strong as you might think. Try cooking it whole, as in the recipe on page 66, or make it into superb faggots. Venison kidneys, too, are good in faggots. Ask your butcher if he knows a source of venison offal, or check online.

Some deer liver can be infected with flukes (a parasite) so always check your source is reputable and that the meat has gone through the proper safety checks.

Whole Roast Venison Liver

Venison liver is highly prized and to my mind one of the best of all livers, with a beautifully sweet but not strong flavour. It's not that easy to find, unless you know a friendly gamekeeper, but there are some online suppliers and it's well worth hunting out.

Serves 2

1	whole venison liver (400–500g)
100g	caul fat
1 tbsp	Dijon mustard
1 tbsp	each of chopped parsley, chives, tarragon and chervil
2 tbsp	vegetable oil
2 tbsp	butter
1	shallot, peeled and sliced
2 tbsp	brandy
1 tsp	redcurrant jelly
200ml	veal stock
1 tsp	English mustard
1 tbsp	crème fraiche
	salt and freshly ground black pepper

Trim any veins, gristle or thick silver skin away from the liver, then pat it dry with kitchen paper.

Rinse the caul fat in cold water and spread it out on your work surface.

Brush the liver with the Dijon mustard, then dust the entire surface with the chopped herbs and season with salt and pepper. Place the liver on the caul, wrap it up and trim off any excess. Tie the caul in place with some butcher's string.

Preheat the oven to 200°C/Fan 180°C/Gas 6. Heat the oil in a roasting tin on the hob, add a tablespoon of the butter, then brown the liver on all sides. Place the tin in the oven and roast the liver for about 10 minutes by which time it should feel firm to the touch. I prefer my liver pink, but it's up to you. Remove the liver when done to your taste and leave it to rest in a warm place.

Discard the fat from the tin and add the remaining tablespoon of butter. Put the tin on the hob, add the sliced shallot and sweat until tender, then add the brandy and jelly. Pour in the stock and simmer until you have a syrupy, gravy-like sauce, scraping any caramelised morsels from the bottom of the tin. Whisk in the English mustard and crème fraiche to finish.

Slice the liver and serve it with the sauce and some roasted root vegetables.

Venison Faggots

This is another good way of preparing venison liver if you've been lucky enough to get hold of some.

Serves 4

400g	venison liver
150g	lardo (cured pork fat), diced
200g	pork belly, diced
	grating of nutmeg
	brandy
1 tbsp	butter
2	onions, peeled and finely chopped
3	garlic cloves, peeled and finely chopped
3 tbsp	chopped flatleaf parsley
1 tbsp	picked thyme leaves
200g	caul fat
	salt and freshly ground black pepper

Trim any veins, gristle or thick silver skin away from the liver and pat it dry with some kitchen paper.

Dice the liver, then mix it with the lardo and pork belly in a bowl. Season liberally with salt, pepper and nutmeg, add a splash of brandy, then leave the meat to marinate for 2 hours.

Melt the butter in a frying pan, add the onions and garlic and cook them very gently until soft and translucent. Remove the pan from the heat and set the onion and garlic aside to cool.

Once the meat has marinated, put it through a mincer with a medium plate – the mince shouldn't be too fine. Beat in the cooled onion and garlic and the herbs.

Preheat the oven to 200°C/Fan 180°/Gas 6. Rinse the caul fat in cold water and lay it out on your work surface. Shape the minced meat into 8 balls and place them on the caul fat, spacing them out evenly. Wrap each faggot in caul fat, cutting the caul as you go. Put the faggots in an ovenproof dish with the edges of the caul tucked underneath them.

Cook the faggots in the preheated oven for 25–30 minutes, basting them with the fat and juices in the dish at least a couple of times to keep them moist. Serve with a nice selection of wild mushrooms.

Pickled Venison Heart

Pickling was once an important means of preserving meat for the lean times of the year. We don't need to do that nowadays, but this spicy, pickled heart is still well worth trying, as it makes a nice tasty morsel to serve as a snack or with drinks.

Serves 6

1	venison heart
½ tbsp	salt
½ tsp	black peppercorns
1 tbsp	brown sugar
3	small sweet onions, peeled and finely sliced
1	dried chilli
4	allspice berries
½ blade	mace
1 tsp	sea salt
	cider vinegar

Trim any excess fat or sinew away from the top of the heart. Place the heart in a saucepan of cold water and bring it to the boil. Skim any scum from the surface, season with the salt, peppercorns and the brown sugar, then simmer gently for 35–40 minutes until tender. Drain the heart and leave it to cool.

Once the heart is cold, cut it into chunks and mix with the sliced onions.

Take a sterilised 750ml preserving jar and place the meat and onions inside. Half-fill the jar with 350ml of cold water, then add the chilli, allspice berries, mace and sea salt. Fill the jar to the top with cider vinegar and seal. Shake well to mix all the ingredients.

Place the jar in the fridge and leave the heart for 4 or 5 days before eating.

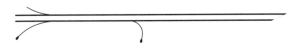

Game and Cep Tartine

I like to freeze the hearts and livers of any partridge, pheasant, wild ducks and grouse that I cook, then when I have enough I make this dish. It's a real treat and also makes a nice garnish for roasted game. If you don't have quite enough game bird innards you can always add a few chicken or duck livers and hearts.

Serves 4

1	egg
200ml	whole milk
	freshly grated nutmeg
4 slices	sourdough bread (about 2cm thick)
400g	game bird livers and hearts
6	medium ceps, cleaned
1	shallot, peeled and finely chopped
1	garlic clove, peeled and finely chopped
	leaves from a sprig of thyme
1 tbsp	butter
1½ tbsp	vegetable oil
	salt and freshly ground black pepper

Beat the egg in a bowl, add the milk, then season with a little salt and pepper and a generous grating of nutmeg. Dip the bread slices in this mixture, leaving them long enough to soften but not allowing them to lose their shape. Remove the bread and set it aside.

Trim the livers, removing any green bits, then chop the livers and hearts quite finely. Chop 2 of the ceps and add them to the meat with the shallot, garlic and thyme. Mix well and season with salt and pepper. Using a spoon or a palette knife, spread the mixture over the slices of bread.

Melt the butter and half a tablespoon of the oil in a pan until foaming, then carefully place the slices offal-side down in the pan. Cook them for 6–7 minutes over a medium heat, then flip them over and continue to cook until browned and crisp. Heat the rest of the oil in a separate pan. Cut the remaining ceps into quarters and fry them in the remaining tablespoon of oil.

Serve the tartines topped with the ceps and perhaps a parsley salad on the side.

Pheasant Liver Turnovers

If you like cooking pheasant, keep all the livers in the freezer until you have enough to make these excellent little turnovers. Alternatively, ask your butcher or local gamekeeper if they can order some livers for you. You can also use partridge livers.

Serves 6 as a starter or snack

1 tbsp	vegetable oil
1	shallot, peeled and finely chopped
2	garlic cloves, peeled and finely chopped
2 tbsp	brandy
4	juniper berries, chopped
600g	pheasant livers
100g	lardo (cured pork fat)
	flour, for dusting
400g	puff pastry
1	egg, beaten
	flaked sea salt
	black pepper

Heat the oil in a frying pan, add the shallot and garlic and sweat them gently over a medium heat until translucent. Add the brandy and the juniper berries, then remove the pan from the heat and set it aside to cool.

Chop the livers and the lardo (not too fine) and put them in a bowl, then add the shallot and garlic mixture. Season lightly and mix well.

Preheat the oven to 210°C/Fan 190°Fan/Gas 6½. Dust your work surface with flour and roll out the puff pastry to a thickness of about 3mm. Divide the pastry into rectangles measuring 24 x 12cm.

Lightly brush the edges of one of the rectangles with beaten egg and place about 2 tablespoons of the liver mixture on one side. Fold the pastry over the filling and press firmly to seal the edges and make an oblong turnover. Brush with beaten egg and score with the tip of a knife to decorate, then sprinkle with black pepper and flaked sea salt. Repeat with the remaining pastry and filling.

Place the turnovers on a baking sheet and cook them in the preheated oven for 20 minutes. Delicious hot or cold.

Pigeon Offal Pie

You can make pigeon pie with just pigeon meat, but using the offal and additional chicken livers, as in this recipe, brings a wonderful gamey flavour.

Serves 6

2	whole pigeons, with hearts, livers and gizzards
1	small savoy cabbage
2 tbsp	olive oil
75g	ventreche or unsmoked streaky bacon, cut into small lardons
	brandy
200ml	veal stock
8	chicken livers (about 180g)
80g	foie gras, diced
2	shallots, peeled and finely chopped
2 sprigs	thyme
350g	puff pastry
	flour, for dusting
2	egg yolks, beaten
	salt and freshly ground black pepper

Bone the pigeons and remove the skin – or ask your butcher to do this for you. Cut the breasts into 8 pieces. Trim the hearts and cut them in half and clean the gizzards, cutting each into 6 pieces. Set the livers aside with the chicken livers.

Remove the outside 4 or 5 leaves of the cabbage and cut out the cores. Blanch the leaves in salted, boiling water until tender, refresh in iced water, then drain and pat them dry on a cloth. Set them aside.

Thinly slice the remaining cabbage. Place a shallow pan over a medium heat with a tablespoon of the olive oil. Add the bacon and fry until lightly browned. Add the sliced cabbage and sweat it with the bacon for 2–3 minutes. Add a splash of brandy, season with salt and pepper and add the stock. Bring to the boil, then reduce the heat. Cook uncovered for 8–10 minutes until the cabbage is cooked through. Then increase the heat and boil rapidly for 1 minute, stirring constantly, to reduce any remaining liquid to a glaze. Set aside.

Heat a frying pan over a high heat, season the chicken and pigeon livers and the foie gras and sauté them quickly in the hot pan. Once the livers have some colour, add the shallots, thyme and a good splash of brandy. Remove the pan from the heat while the livers are still pink. Pass the hot mixture through a fine sieve into a bowl, keeping all of the fat and liquid. Season well with freshly ground pepper and set aside.

Season the pigeon meat, hearts and gizzards. Heat a tablespoon of oil in a frying pan and when it's very hot, sear the pigeon meat, hearts and gizzards until coloured on the outside but very pink inside. Set them aside.

Roll out the pastry on a floured work surface to 3mm thick. Cut out a 22cm circle and a 26cm circle and put the larger piece back in the fridge.

Place the smaller circle on a baking sheet lined with greaseproof paper. Use a knife to mark a border 1.5cm in from the edge.

Place a layer of the blanched cabbage leaves on the inner circle of the pastry. Spread a third of the liver mixture on top and then half of the cabbage and bacon. Add another third of the liver, then lay the hearts, meat and gizzards in a circle on top, working slightly inwards to start to form a dome shape. Top with the rest of the cabbage and finish the dome with the final third of liver mixture. Cover the dome with the remaining blanched cabbage leaves to encase everything.

Brush the edges of the pastry with egg yolk. Take the second pastry circle and lay it over the top to cover the pie. Press the edges well to seal and trim the circle neatly. Chill the pie for at least 30 minutes.

Brush the outside of the pie with the remaining egg yolk, then put it back in the fridge for 10 minutes. Preheat the oven to 220°C/Fan 200°C/Gas 7. If you like, use a knife to mark a pattern on the pastry.

Bake in the hot oven for 12 minutes, then turn down the heat to 200°C/Fan 180°C/Gas 6 and cook for another 35 minutes until the pie is a beautiful deep golden brown colour. Remove it from the oven and leave it to rest for 20 minutes before serving.

LES
COCHONNAILLES

LES COCHONNAILLES: *pork meats – every bit of the pig*

The pig is the true hero of nose-to-tail eating. You really can eat everything, from the snout right down to the curly tail! It is the most versatile of all the animals we consume and its meat can be cooked, cured, preserved, air-dried, salted – the possibilities are endless. We even use the blood in boudin noir or black pudding as well as in blood pancakes – much loved by my late father-in-law.

In France and other parts of Europe the pig is considered so special that whole shops – charcuterie – are devoted to the craft of using all parts of the pig to make not only sausages and salamis but also dishes such as terrines and caillettes (the French version of faggots).

In the old days a family would keep a pig in the backyard and it would eat anything it was given and be content. When time came to kill the animal the family would feed off it for months, preparing and preserving the meat in so many ways and wasting nothing.

Nowadays most of us don't keep our own pig, but we are becoming accustomed once again to eating more of the animal and wasting less. Pig's ears, crispy tails and even the pig's head are appearing on the menus of many restaurants, and people are relearning the skills of making terrines and brawn. And gone are the days when pork was just pork. Now we can choose our favourite breed – mine is Middle White. We recognise the variations in flavour and the difference in the quality of the offal too.

The recipes in this chapter celebrate the incredible bounty of this animal and I hope they will encourage you to branch out from pork chops. Enjoy!

Boudin Noir Ravioli with Bone Marrow Broth

I like to make these ravioli with boudin noir rather than black pudding, as it is softer and creamier in texture. However, they will work with any good quality black pudding. My preference is to make large ravioli and serve one per person, but you can vary the size and shape as you like.

Serves 4

1	boudin noir (about 120g)
1 litre	veal or chicken stock
1 tbsp	sherry vinegar
100g	bone marrow, soaked in cold water for an hour and cut into cubes
3 tbsp	chopped flatleaf parsley
	Dijon mustard
	salt and freshly ground black pepper

Pasta

150g	strong white flour, plus extra for dusting
1	egg
1	egg yolk
1 tsp	olive oil
	pinch of salt

First make the pasta. Put all the ingredients in a food processor and blitz until the mixture is the texture of wet crumbs. You may need to add a drop of water, depending on the size of your eggs. Tip the dough out and knead it into a ball for 2 or 3 minutes, then wrap it in cling film and leave it in the fridge for 30 minutes to rest.

Dust your work surface with flour and roll out the pasta. Pass it through a pasta roller, gradually bringing it to the thinnest setting.

Cut out 8 circles from the pasta. Divide the boudin noir into 4. Place a piece on one of the circles, moisten the edges of the pasta and place another circle on top. Seal the edges tight, making sure there are no air pockets. Repeat with the remaining boudin and pasta. Set the ravioli aside on a floured plate until you're ready to cook.

Bring the stock to the boil and cook it for 20 minutes to reduce it slightly and intensify the flavour. You should be left with about 600ml. Season the stock well and add the sherry vinegar.

Cook the ravioli in a large pan of salted, boiling water, then drain. Bring the stock back to the boil, add the cubes of bone marrow and simmer for 2 minutes. Take the pan off the heat, add the pasta and chopped parsley and very gently and carefully toss them together.

Serve the ravioli in bowls. First smear the base of each bowl with a teaspoon of Dijon mustard. Gently add the ravioli on top with some of the rich marrow stock.

Black Pudding with Chestnuts

Black pudding isn't hard to make and it is so good. This is a perfect breakfast feast, served with fried eggs and some home-made green tomato relish (see page 248).

Makes 16 slices

1	pig's tongue
	salt
180g	lardo (cured pork fat)
500ml	pig's blood
2 tbsp	lard
2	large onions, peeled and finely chopped
2 tbsp	fresh breadcrumbs
2 tbsp	chopped flatleaf parsley
¼ tsp	freshly grated nutmeg
¼ tsp	ground cinnamon
½ tsp	chilli powder
½ tsp	white pepper
1	egg, beaten
120g	chestnuts, cooked, peeled and broken up
	flour, for dusting
1 tbsp	vegetable oil, for frying

Place the tongue in a saucepan of cold water, add a handful of salt and bring to the boil. Turn down the heat, then simmer the tongue for 2½ hours until tender. Leave it to cool, then peel off the membrane.

Mince the tongue with the pork fat, then whisk in the blood. Make sure to keep everything very cold.

Preheat the oven to 180°C/Fan 160°C/Gas 4. Melt the lard in a frying pan, add the onions and sweat them until completely cooked. Don't let them brown. Tip them into a bowl and add the breadcrumbs, parsley, spices, white pepper and 12 grams of salt. When the mixture is completely cool, add the beaten egg, blood and tongue mixture and the chestnuts.

Pour everything into a greased terrine or loaf tin and cover with a piece of foil. Place the terrine in a roasting tin and pour hot water into the tin to a depth of 4cm, then cook in the preheated oven for 1½ hours. Remove and leave to cool, then chill the pudding in the fridge overnight. It will keep for up to 2 weeks.

To serve, turn the black pudding out of the tin and cut into slices. Dust the slices in flour and fry gently on both sides in a little oil to warm through.

White Pudding Terrine

You can put the white pudding into sausage skins if you like or just pour the mixture into a tin and bake it: much easier and simpler and the taste is just as good.

Makes 20 slices

2	pig's tongues
200g	pork skin
1	onion, peeled and cut in half
1	celery stick
1	bay leaf
360g	skinless chicken breasts, cut into cubes
200g	pork mince
180g	pork fat, diced
2 tbsp	butter, plus extra for greasing
2	shallots, peeled and chopped
2 tbsp	port
360g	double cream
1 tbsp	thyme leaves
160g	fresh white breadcrumbs
	grated nutmeg
1	egg, beaten
	salt and freshly ground black pepper

If possible, buy brined tongues as they have a lovely pink colour, but fresh ones will do. Rinse the tongues well in cold water, put them in the pan with the skin and cover generously with cold water. Add salt, then the onion, celery and bay leaf and bring to the boil. Turn the heat down and simmer for 1½–2 hours until tender. Leave to cool.

Peel the membrane off the tongues and cut the meat into large dice. Dice the skin and put everything in the fridge until needed. Put the chicken, pork mince and pork fat in the freezer for an hour to get very cold.

Melt the butter in a saucepan and sweat the shallots until translucent. Add the port, followed by the cream, bring to the boil and immediately take the pan off the heat. Add the thyme and breadcrumbs and season with nutmeg and plenty of salt and pepper. Cover the pan and leave to cool. Butter a terrine or loaf tin.

Preheat the oven to 180°/Fan 160°C/Gas 4. Put the chicken, pork mince and pork fat into a food processor. Blitz for about 30 seconds, then add the shallot and cream mix and the egg. Continue to blitz until smooth – this should take about 2 minutes. Fold in the diced skin and tongue and pour everything into the terrine or loaf tin. Cover with foil and place the terrine in a roasting tin. Add hot water to come 3cm up the sides of the terrine and bake for 2 hours.

Remove the white pudding from the oven and leave it to cool, then refrigerate overnight. To serve, cut the white pudding into slices of about 2cm thick and fry them in a little butter. Serve in the same way as black pudding.

Gratin of Andouillette

Not everyone likes these French sausages, andouillettes, but for others they are the height of deliciousness. The taste and seasoning varies from region to region and some are mild, made with veal, while others use pork and are much stronger. My personal favourites are from the Charcuterie Bobosse in Lyon. His classic 'tirée à la ficelle' are mild in taste and great grilled, but here I use them in a gratin. This is classic Lyonnaise cooking.

Serves 4

2	andouillette sausages
1 tbsp	butter
2	garlic cloves, peeled and chopped
2	shallots, peeled and chopped
100g	button mushrooms, washed and sliced
100ml	dry white wine
200ml	whipping cream
2 tbsp	crème fraiche
1 tbsp	Dijon mustard
2 tbsp	breadcrumbs
2 tbsp	grated Gruyère cheese
	salt and freshly ground black pepper

Preheat the oven to 180°C/Fan 160°C/Gas 4. Remove the andouillette meat from the casings, chop it coarsely and set it aside.

Melt the butter in a sauté pan and add the garlic, shallots and mushrooms. Sweat them until soft, then add the wine and a little seasoning. Bring to the boil, then add the whipping cream and crème fraiche and simmer for 5 minutes.

Take the pan off the heat and mix in the chopped andouillette and the mustard. Tip the mixture into a big ovenproof dish or 4 individual ones.

Mix the breadcrumbs and cheese and sprinkle them over the top, then bake the gratin in the preheated oven for 10 minutes until bubbling. If the top isn't golden, put the dish or dishes under a hot grill for a couple of minutes. Serve at once.

Cassoulet Terrine

This is a wonderful terrine made with pig's trotters, beans and sausage – all the flavours of a cassoulet. You do need a really good meaty sausage for this recipe, with 100 per cent pork and no filler. Morteau, a lightly smoked, very flavoursome sausage, is perfect, but failing that a Toulouse or good garlic sausage works well. Long trotters, by the way, are the back feet of the pig and those are the ones you need here.

Serves 16

2	long pig's trotters
200g	white beans, soaked in cold water overnight
1	carrot, peeled
1	onion, peeled
2	celery sticks
1 tsp	black peppercorns
120g	good-quality sausage (preferably Morteau, Toulouse or garlic)
1 tbsp	olive oil
2	shallots, peeled and chopped
100g	Alsace bacon, cut into lardons
400ml	veal stock
2	gelatine leaves, soaked in cold water
8	plum tomatoes, peeled, deseeded and chopped
	salt and freshly ground black pepper

Scrape any marks from the trotters and singe off any hairs with a blowtorch. Rinse the trotters well.

Place the soaked beans, carrot, onion and celery in a large saucepan and add water to cover. Add the trotters and season with salt and the black peppercorns. Bring the water to the boil, skim, then reduce the heat and simmer for 2 hours, adding the sausage for the last 20 minutes. You may need to top up with boiling water. At the end of the 2 hours the beans should be cooked and the trotters tender. Remove the pan from the heat and leave everything to cool.

Heat the oil in a separate large pan and gently cook the chopped shallots. Don't allow them to colour. Add the bacon and cook for another 5 minutes, then add the veal stock and cook until it's reduced by half. Squeeze the excess water from the gelatine leaves, add them to the pan and remove the pan from the heat. Stir in the chopped tomatoes.

Remove the trotters and the sausage. Take all the bones out of the trotters and chop the meat into 2cm dice. Dice the sausage too. Drain the beans and add them to the bacon mixture along with the diced trotters and sausage. Mix well and season with salt and pepper.

Line a terrine dish or loaf tin with cling film, leaving some overhanging the sides. Spoon the mixture into the dish or tin and fold the cling film over to cover. Place the terrine in the fridge and leave it to chill and set overnight.

Once the terrine has set, remove it from the dish and slice it carefully, using a knife dipped in hot water. Serve with a green salad and cornichons.

Andouille Pastilla with Tomato and Harissa Dressing

Andouille and andouillette are both made from pig and veal offal but andouille are smoked and can be served cold. Here they are used in pastillas, a North African speciality made with brick pastry, which is similar to filo but easier to use and with a better texture. It's available in some supermarkets – look for feuilles de brick or brik. You need good thick slices of andouille.

Serves 4

2 tbsp	plain flour
8 sheets	brick pastry
2 tbsp	Dijon mustard
8 slices	andouille sausage
100g	clarified butter

Tomato and harissa dressing

1	garlic clove, peeled and chopped
250ml	olive oil, plus 1 tbsp
2 tsp	cumin seeds, toasted
½ tsp	harissa paste
6	plum tomatoes, peeled, deseeded and chopped
pinch	saffron
	juice of ½ lemon
	salt and freshly ground black pepper

To make the tomato and harissa dressing, put the garlic in a frying pan with the tablespoon of olive oil and cook it gently for a couple of minutes. Add the cumin seeds and the harissa and mix well, then add the chopped tomato flesh and cook until most of the moisture has evaporated.

Remove the pan from the heat, add the saffron and lemon juice and season with salt. Once the mix has cooled to room temperature, stir in the 250ml of olive oil.

For the pastilla, mix the plain flour with water to form a paste. Lay a sheet of brick pastry on your work surface and spread some mustard in the centre. Add a slice of andouille on top of the mustard. Brush the edges of the pastry with the flour and water paste, then roll it up from the edge nearest to you, folding the sides in before reaching the top edge. Seal the edges together.

Place a frying pan over a medium heat – not too high – and add some clarified butter. Shallow-fry the pastillas in batches until they're golden brown on each side. Put each batch on a baking tray and keep them warm in a low oven until they're all cooked. Serve hot with the tomato and harissa dressing.

Haslet

This is a traditional dish from Lincolnshire and it's basically a meat loaf made from minced offal and wrapped in caul fat. It's excellent eaten thinly sliced with pickles or in sandwiches.

Serves 10–12

400g	pork belly
300g	pig's liver
120g	white bread
150ml	milk
1 tbsp	butter, plus extra for greasing
½	large onion, peeled and chopped
good pinch	ground nutmeg
good pinch	ground allspice
4	sage leaves, chopped
1 tsp	picked and chopped thyme leaves
1 tbsp	chopped flatleaf parsley
1	egg, beaten
	caul fat
	salt and freshly ground black pepper

Cut the pork belly and pig's liver into large dice. Soak the bread in the milk to soften it.

Melt the butter in a frying pan and add the chopped onion. Cook the onion gently for 5–6 minutes, but don't allow it to colour. Remove the pan from the heat and leave the onion to cool.

Put the pork belly and liver through the fine plate of a mincer and place them in a large mixing bowl. Season with salt, pepper, nutmeg and allspice, then add the soaked bread, the chopped herbs, beaten egg and the cooled onion. Mix well. Preheat the oven to 180°C/Fan 160°C/Gas 4.

Take a small amount of the mixture and wrap it in a piece of buttered foil. Put it in the oven to cook for 4 or 5 minutes, then taste to check the seasoning. Add more salt and pepper as required.

Butter an ovenproof terrine or loaf tin (about 20cm by 15cm by 8cm). Lay the caul fat in the terrine or tin, letting it hang over the edges. Spoon in the pork mixture and fold the caul fat over the top.

Place the haslet in the preheated oven and cook it for 1 hour and 15 minutes. Remove it from the oven and leave to cool. Once the haslet is cool enough, put it in the fridge overnight. The next day, turn it out of the terrine or tin and serve with pickles or chutney.

Home-cured Brawn

Brawn is also known as 'head cheese' and is indeed made from a pig's head and set with the gelatinous cooking liquid. It's great for a party or buffet, as it serves lots of people, but it keeps well and is a lovely thing to have in the fridge and enjoy for lunches and snacks over a week or so. It's quite a long process but well worth it. Saltpetre, or potassium nitrate, is a special salt used for curing meat and should be handled with care.

Serves at least 16 as a starter

1	pig's head, boned
500g	sea salt
1 tbsp	cracked black and white peppercorns
1 sprig	thyme
1 tsp	saltpetre
1 tbsp	sugar
2	onions, peeled
2	carrots, peeled
2	celery sticks, washed
1	bouquet garni
1 bottle	white wine
4	shallots, peeled and finely chopped
2 tbsp	wholegrain mustard
2 tbsp	chopped parsley
	salt and freshly ground black pepper

Clean and scrape the pig's head and burn off any hairs with a blowtorch. Mix together the sea salt, peppercorns, thyme, saltpetre and sugar.

Rub the salt mix into both sides of the head, then lay it on a tray and cover with cling film. Leave the head in the fridge for 10 days, turning it after 5 days.

After 10 days remove the head from the tray and rinse it under running water for 10 minutes.

Place the head in a large saucepan and cover it with fresh water. Bring the water to the boil and skim well, then add the vegetables, bouquet garni and half the white wine. Turn the heat down and simmer the head gently for 3½ hours until it's tender.

Remove the pan from the heat and leave everything to cool slightly. Remove the head and vegetables from the pan, then pass the liquid through a sieve and set it aside. Cut the carrots, onions and celery into 1cm dice and the meat from the head into 2cm dice. Place the vegetables and meat in a large bowl.

Put the chopped shallots in a pan, add the rest of the wine and cook over a high heat until the wine is reduced by half. Add 1.4 litres of the reserved cooking liquid, bring it to the boil and cook for 5–6 minutes to reduce it.

Pour the liquid over the meat and vegetables and add the mustard and chopped parsley. Stir, then season well. You can leave the brawn in the bowl or pour it into a terrine. Cover it and place it in the fridge overnight to set. It will keep for at least a week.

Pig's Cheeks in Jelly

This is a very rustic, meaty terrine – similar to jellied rillettes. It makes a great starter and is perfect for picnics. You can make this in one big bowl or in individual ones.

Serves 6

2 litres	cider
200g	coarse sea salt
50g	soft brown sugar
1 blade	mace
10	black peppercorns
8	large pig's cheeks
1	celery stick, roughly chopped
1	onion, peeled and cut into wedges
1	carrot, peeled and roughly chopped
2	bay leaves
1 sprig	thyme
5	allspice berries
1	clove
2	gelatine leaves, softened in cold water
1 bunch	flatleaf parsley, chopped
1	garlic clove, peeled and finely chopped
½ tbsp	red wine vinegar
	salt and freshly ground black pepper

Put the cider, salt, sugar, mace and black peppercorns in a saucepan and bring to the boil. Remove the pan from the heat and leave to cool.

Once the brine has cooled, pour it into a bowl, add the cheeks and cover. Put the cheeks in the fridge for 4 days, turning them every day. On the fourth day, remove the cheeks from the brine and put them in a bowl of fresh water. Leave them in the fridge overnight.

Place the cheeks in a saucepan, cover them with cold water and bring to a simmer. Taste the water to check that it isn't too salty. If it is, change for fresh water and return to a simmer. Add the celery, onion, carrot, bay, thyme, allspice and clove, then simmer for about 1½ hours, uncovered. Remove the pan from the heat and leave the cheeks to cool in the liquid.

Once the cheeks are cool, remove them and set the liquid aside. Shred the meat into a bowl. Take 500ml of the cooking liquid and pass it through a sieve into a clean pan, skimming off any fat. Place the pan over a low heat and warm the liquid gently. Add the softened gelatine and let it dissolve, then add the chopped parsley, garlic and red wine vinegar. Check the seasoning of the liquid and add salt and pepper if needed, then stir it into the cheek meat. Cover the bowl with cling film and place it in the fridge for the mixture to set.

The next day, turn the mixture out and slice or just scoop out helpings as you like. Serve with warm toast or bread and pickles.

Pork Faggots

*Faggots are cheap to make and great to eat. They used to be
very popular in Britain and have recently been coming back
into favour. Some good butchers make their own. Pig's liver
and kidney is easy to get but if you can't find heart, just use
extra liver and kidney instead.*

Makes 8 faggots

600g	pig's liver, kidney and heart
300g	pork belly without skin
300g	pork fat
120g	spinach, chard or dandelion leaves, washed
2 tbsp	olive oil
2	onions, peeled and chopped
2	garlic cloves, peeled and chopped
pinch	ground mace
1 tbsp	chopped parsley
1 tbsp	coarsely chopped sage
360g	caul fat
	salt and freshly ground black pepper

Trim the liver, kidney and heart of any sinew, then mince it with the belly and fat. Put it all in a bowl.

Bring a pan of salted water to the boil, blanch the washed leaves for 30 seconds, then refresh them in iced water. Drain the leaves and squeeze them dry. Roughly chop the leaves and add them to the meat.

Heat the oil in a frying pan and sweat the onion and garlic until soft. Leave to cool, then add them to the meat. Add the mace and herbs and season well.

Rinse the caul fat in cold water and then lay it out on your work surface. Divide the meat into 8 balls, place them on the caul, spacing them at regular intervals. Cut around each faggot and wrap it tightly in caul. Preheat the oven to 200°C/ Fan 180°C/Gas 6.

Put the wrapped faggots in a roasting tin and cook them in the preheated oven for 40 minutes. Remove and leave them to rest for 10 minutes before serving. Coleslaw (see page 242) is an excellent accompaniment.

Stuffed Cabbage with Pig's Liver and Buckwheat

There are many recipes for stuffed cabbage, but this Polish version is a particular favourite of mine. It's a good hearty winter dish and great eaten hot or cold. Buckwheat is an excellent food and nutritious. You need whole buckwheat grains for this, not buckwheat flour.

Serves 6

200g	buckwheat grain
360g	pig's liver
1	small savoy cabbage
30g	lard
120g	smoked bacon, diced
2	onions, peeled and sliced
1 litre	veal or beef stock
	salt and freshly ground black pepper

Rinse the buckwheat, put it in a saucepan of cold water and bring it to the boil. Cook for 20-30 minutes or until tender, then drain and leave to cool. Trim any sinew off the pork liver, mince the liver and put it in the fridge until needed.

Remove the outer leaves of cabbage and discard them. Take 12 nice big leaves and blanch them in a pan of salted water for 3 minutes. Drain them and refresh them in a bowl of iced water, then lay them flat on a clean tea towel or some kitchen paper to dry. Cut out the thickest part of the stalk of each leaf. Finely shred the heart of the cabbage.

Melt the lard in a large pan and add the bacon. Gently fry the bacon until it's just starting to colour, then add the shredded cabbage and sliced onions. Sweat them for 20-30 minutes until the cabbage is completely cooked, then tip it all into a bowl and leave to cool.

Once the cabbage mixture is cool, add the liver and buckwheat, season and mix well. Preheat the oven to 200°C/Fan 180°C/Gas 6.

Divide the stuffing between the cabbage leaves. Shape each portion into a ball, wrap it up in a cabbage leaf and place the stuffed leaf in an ovenproof dish or baking tin, seam-side down. The stuffed leaves should be touching and a close fit so they stay in place.

Pour over the stock, then cover the dish with foil. Bake in the oven for 20 minutes, then remove the foil and cook for another 30 minutes. The cooking juices are delicious, so spoon some over each helping when you serve this dish.

Crispy Pig's Ears

*These crispy, salty morsels make the most delightful snack.
You can do all the boiling the day before you want to serve
them, then just fry them at the last minute and add any
seasoning you like. Paprika, chilli and cumin are all great.*

Serves 4 as a snack

6	pig's ears
1	onion, peeled and roughly chopped
1	celery stick, roughly chopped
1	carrot, peeled and roughly chopped
1	bay leaf
1 sprig	thyme
pinch	whole peppercorns
	potato flour, for dusting
	sea salt

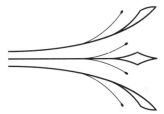

Scrape the ears to remove any marks and burn off any hairs with a blowtorch. Rinse the ears well, place them in a large saucepan and cover them with cold water. Bring the water to the boil, skim, then add the vegetables, herbs and peppercorns. Turn down the heat and simmer the ears for about 2 hours or until tender. Remove the pan from the heat and leave the ears to cool in the liquid.

Once the ears are cool, remove them from the pan and put them on a baking tray. Cover them with greaseproof paper and put another same-sized tray on top. Weigh the tray down with a couple of cans to press the ears slightly. Put them in the fridge until completely cold and set.

Half-fill a large saucepan with vegetable oil and heat it to 170°C. Cut the cold ears into long thin strips and dust them with potato flour. Fry them, a few at a time, until crispy – take care as the oil may spit as you add the ears. Drain the fried ears on kitchen paper and season them with sea salt.

Crispy Pig's Head Wontons

Pig's head makes excellent wontons and if you can get your butcher to bone the head for you, the rest of the work is fairly straightforward. The wontons freeze well so it's worth making lots and stashing some away for another day.

Makes 30–40

½	pig's head, off the bone
500g	pork skin
1 tsp	black peppercorns
2	onions, peeled and chopped into wedges
2	carrots, peeled and quartered
2	celery sticks, broken into large pieces
1	bouquet garni
50g	butter
4	shallots, peeled and finely chopped
2	garlic cloves, peeled and finely chopped
50ml	white wine
3 tbsp	chopped flatleaf parsley
	wonton wrappers
1	egg yolk, beaten
	vegetable oil, for deep-frying
	chilli salt

Scrape the head and skin and singe off any hairs with a blowtorch. Rinse the head and skin, then place them in a large saucepan and cover with cold water. Bring the water to the boil and skim the surface. Season with salt and the peppercorns, add the vegetables and bouquet garni, then reduce the heat to a simmer. Cook for 3 hours or until the head is very tender. Leave it to cool in the liquid – overnight is fine.

In a separate pan, melt the butter and add the chopped shallots. Cook them gently for 6–8 minutes until translucent but don't allow them to colour. At this point, add the garlic, cook for a further 2 minutes, then add the white wine. Continue to cook until the wine is reduced by three quarters, then tip everything into a bowl.

Remove the cooked head and skin from the cooking liquid and dice it all – the pieces should be roughly 1cm. Add the meat to the shallot and garlic mixture, season well and add the chopped parsley. Leave the mixture to cool.

To make the wontons, take a wrapper and brush the edges with a little egg yolk. Place a small spoonful of the mixture in the centre and fold the wrapper over to form a triangle. Press the edges together firmly. Brush a little egg yolk on the two opposite corners of the triangle and pinch them together. Repeat until you have used all the mixture.

Half-fill a large saucepan or a deep-fat fryer with vegetable oil and heat it to 180°C. Fry the wontons in batches until golden brown and crisp. Drain them on kitchen paper, season with chilli salt and serve.

If you like, you can freeze some of the wontons once cooled. They can then be fried from frozen.

Pig's Snout, Ear and Tail Stew

Yes, you can even eat a pig's snout, which is particularly prized for its flavour and texture. In this recipe the snout is cooked with the ears and tail to make an excellent stew.

Serves 4

1	pig's snout
2	pig's ears
1	pig's tail
2	onions, peeled
1	celery stick, roughly chopped
1	carrot, peeled and roughly chopped
1	bay leaf
1 sprig	thyme
3 tbsp	olive oil
2	garlic cloves, finely chopped
3	plum tomatoes, peeled, deseeded and diced
500g	broad beans, podded and skinned
	salt and freshly ground black pepper

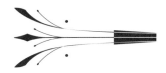

Scrape the snout, ears and tail to remove any marks and burn off any hairs with a blowtorch. Rinse everything well, place in a large saucepan and cover with cold water. Bring the water to the boil, skim, then add one of the onions, roughly chopped, the celery, carrot, herbs and a good pinch of salt. Turn down the heat and simmer for about 2 hours or until tender – the ears will still have a little crunch to them from the cartilage but this is all part of the textural sensation of the dish. Remove the pan from the heat and leave everything to cool in the liquid.

Heat the oil in a large saucepan over a medium heat. Finely chop the remaining onion and sauté it in the oil until golden brown. Add the garlic and cook for a minute, then add the tomatoes and cook until the liquid all evaporates and the sauce thickens.

Cut all the meat into bite-sized pieces, removing the bones from the tail. Add the meat to the pan to warm through, then add the broad beans and simmer until the beans are cooked. Serve hot with some crusty bread to mop up the juices.

Pig's Trotter Terrine

*Eating trotters is all about appreciating their gelatinous texture –
something that is much more favoured in China and Japan than
in most of Europe. This terrine is a classic, found in charcuteries
the length and breadth of France, but it's easy to make at home
once you've done the brining and boiling, which does take a
while. Long trotters, by the way, are the back feet of the pig.*

Serves 8–12

6	long pig's trotters, split in half
250g	coarse sea salt
50g	caster sugar
1 tsp	cracked black pepper
1 tsp	allspice
1 tsp	cracked juniper berries
1	onion, peeled and cut in half
1	large carrot, peeled
3	garlic cloves, peeled
1 sprig	thyme
2	bay leaves
300ml	dry white wine
12	cornichons, chopped
2 tbsp	chopped flatleaf parsley
1 tbsp	Dijon mustard

Remove any hairs from the trotters with a blowtorch, then scrape off any burnt bits. Rinse the trotters and place them on a baking tray. Mix together the salt, sugar and spices and spread the mixture over the trotters. Rub and massage it into the trotters well, cover them with cling film and refrigerate for 3 days, turning them every day. After the third day, rinse the trotters and discard the brining mixture.

Place the trotters in a large saucepan with the onion, carrot, garlic, thyme and bay leaves. Add the wine and then enough cold water to cover the trotters generously. Bring to the boil, then immediately turn the heat down to a very gentle simmer and skim off any impurities that have risen to the surface.

Continue to simmer for 2 hours – the liquid shouldn't be allowed to boil or it will go cloudy. After 2 hours, check the trotters with a skewer. The meat and tendons should be very tender and falling off the bone. If not, continue to cook, topping up the pan with hot water if necessary. Once the trotters are cooked, leave them to cool in the liquid, then drain, keeping the carrot and the liquid.

Pick all the meat, skin and tendons off the bone, chop it coarsely and put it into a bowl. Chop the reserved carrot and add it to the meat with the cornichons, chopped parsley and mustard.

Finally, add about half of the cooking liquid to the bowl, just enough to moisten the mixture to a loose porridge texture.

Line a terrine dish or a 2-litre pudding basin with cling film. Pour in the terrine mixture, cover with cling film or foil and put it in the fridge for 24 hours. To serve, turn the terrine out of the dish or bowl and slice it very thinly using a hot, very sharp knife and serve with salad leaves. This terrine keeps in the fridge for about 10 days.

Braised Pig's Trotters with White Beans

This is a really hearty dish. It's similar to a cassoulet but uses only trotters so it's cheap to make and satisfying to eat.

Serves 6

6	long pig's trotters
500g	dried white beans, soaked overnight in cold water
2	onions, peeled and left whole
2	carrots, peeled and left whole
1	celery stick
1	bouquet garni
2	garlic cloves, peeled
1 tsp	black peppercorns
	salt and freshly ground black pepper

Garnish

1 tbsp	olive oil
1	onion, peeled and finely chopped
2	carrots, peeled and sliced into rounds
1	garlic clove, peeled and finely chopped
½ tbsp	tomato paste
6	tomatoes, peeled, deseeded and roughly chopped
3 tbsp	chopped flatleaf parsley
3 tbsp	dried breadcrumbs

Scrape any marks from the trotters and singe off any hairs with a blowtorch. Rinse the trotters well.

Drain the beans, place them in a large saucepan with the trotters, whole vegetables, bouquet garni, garlic and black peppercorns. Add water to cover and season with salt. Bring the water to the boil, skim the surface, then turn the heat down and simmer gently for 2½ hours.

To prepare the garnish, heat the oil in a separate pan and sweat the chopped onion for 3 or 4 minutes. Add the sliced carrot and continue to cook for a further 5 minutes, then add the chopped garlic and tomato paste and mix well.

Once the trotters and beans are cooked, remove the trotters from the pan. Drain the beans, discarding the whole vegetables but reserving all the liquid. Tip the beans into the pan with the cooked carrot, onion and tomato mixture and add enough of the cooking liquid to keep it moist.

Remove the bones from the trotters and chop all the meat and skin. Add this to the beans and heat together gently. Preheat your grill.

Season generously with salt and freshly ground pepper, add the chopped tomatoes and a little more cooking liquid if required. Add the chopped parsley and pour everything into a gratin dish. Sprinkle with breadcrumbs and colour lightly under the hot grill.

Confit Pig's Tails with Spiced Cherries

If you like crackling you'll love this recipe. Once fried, the pieces of confit pig's tail become beautifully crisp and golden and they're perfect with the spiced cherries. You can do all the preparation in advance and just quickly fry the tails when you're ready to serve.

Serves 4

8	pig's tails
200g	coarse sea salt
1.25kg	duck fat
4	garlic cloves
1 sprig	thyme

Spiced cherries

50ml	red wine vinegar
	juice and zest of 1 lemon
2 tbsp	caster sugar
3	star anise
2 tbsp	black peppercorns, crushed
200g	cherries, stoned

Scrape the tails and burn off any hairs with a blowtorch. Place the tails in a shallow dish and cover them with the coarse sea salt, then put them in the fridge for about 2 hours.

Melt the duck fat in a large pan. Wipe the salt off the tails and put them in the pan with the fat. Add the garlic and thyme, bring the fat to a very gentle simmer, then cover with a piece of greaseproof paper. Cook the tails for 90 minutes or until the point of a knife easily pierces the thickest part. Remove the pan from the heat and leave the tails to cool in the fat.

Take the tails out of the fat and carefully lay them on a work surface. Using a sharp knife cut down the entire length of a tail and then gently remove all the bones, leaving the skin intact. Repeat with the rest of the tails.

Place all the boned tails on a baking tray, cover them with cling film and place a similar-sized tray on top. Weigh down the tray with a few cans to flatten the tails, then place it in the fridge for at least 2 hours.

For the cherries, pour the vinegar into a saucepan and add the lemon juice, sugar, star anise and peppercorns. Cook until the mixture is syrupy and just about to caramelise, then add the cherries and lemon zest. Cover the pan and simmer for a few minutes until the cherries are tender, then remove the pan from the heat and leave to cool. Set aside until needed.

When the tails are cold and set, cut them into rectangles and place them in a hot non-stick pan to crisp up the skin – you don't need to add any extra fat. It's best to do this in batches so you don't overcrowd the pan. Serve the bits of crispy pig's tail right away while they're hot, with a bowl of the cherries on the side.

Pig's Head Rolls with Black Mustard Seeds

These pig's head rolls make a great starter for a party but also keep well in the fridge for about 10 days. You could also serve slices with a salad as a main course. Make sure you get a pig's head with the cheeks still intact, plus two extra cheeks.

Serves 12 as a starter

1	pig's head (with cheeks)
2	pig's cheeks
1 tbsp	black mustard seeds, lightly crushed
sprig	thyme, chopped
2	onions, peeled and roughly chopped
2	carrots, peeled and roughly chopped
2	celery sticks, washed
1	bouquet garni
1 tbsp	whole black peppercorns
	olive oil
	salt and freshly ground black pepper

Ask your butcher to bone the head, leaving the cheeks in place, and cut the head in half. Scrape the head to remove any marks and blowtorch any hairs. Remove the ears and put them in the freezer to use another time.

Lay each piece of head on a piece of muslin, skin-side down, and season with salt and pepper. Sprinkle with the crushed mustard seeds and chopped thyme. Place an extra cheek on each piece of head. Roll up each piece of head into a cylinder, then wrap tightly in the muslin cloth. Tie the cloth in place with string at each end and at regular intervals to give an even shape.

Place the 2 rolls in a large saucepan of cold water with the onions, carrots, celery and the bouquet garni and season with salt and the whole peppercorns. Bring to the boil, skim, then reduce the heat and simmer for 2½ hours or until the head is tender. Remove the pan from the heat and leave the rolls to cool in the liquid.

Remove the rolls and discard the liquid. Take off the string and muslin and rewrap the rolls tightly in cling film to set the shape. Place them in the fridge overnight to set completely.

When you're ready to serve, remove the cling film and cut the rolls into slices 1½cm thick. Season both sides with salt and pepper. Heat a little olive oil in a frying pan and carefully fry the slices of head until crispy on both sides.

Crispy Wild Boar Head with Shallot Mayonnaise

Boning a wild boar head is quite a task so if you're not up for it, ask your butcher to do it for you. Once boned, the head should be scraped and singed to remove all the bristles. This dish is particularly sensational with wild boar but also good with an ordinary pig's head.

Serves 10–12

1	wild boar head, boned (2–3kg boned weight)
1	garlic clove, peeled and very finely chopped
1 tbsp	Dijon grain mustard
1 tbsp	mixed chopped rosemary and thyme leaves
1	celery stick
1	carrot, peeled
1	onion, peeled
2	bay leaves
1 tbsp	black peppercorns
1 tbsp	vegetable oil
	salt and freshly ground black pepper

Spicy shallot mayonnaise

2	shallots, peeled and finely chopped
125ml	dry white wine
125ml	veal stock
pinch	cayenne pepper
2	egg yolks
1 tbsp	Dijon mustard
1 tbsp	white wine vinegar
250ml	vegetable oil

Lay the head out flat on your work surface, skin-side down, and season. Mix the garlic, mustard, rosemary and thyme and spread the mixture evenly over the meat. Roll the head up neatly and tie it tightly with string.

Place the head in a large saucepan, cover it generously with cold water and bring it to the boil. Skim well, add the celery, carrot, onion, bay leaves, peppercorns and some salt, then turn down the heat so the water is barely simmering. Cook the head gently for 2–3 hours, depending on the size, until the meat is tender and easily pierced with a skewer. Leave it to cool in the cooking liquid.

Once the head is cool, take it out and roll it tightly in cling film. Refrigerate overnight. Pass the stock through a sieve and use it for a soup another time.

For the sauce, simmer the finely chopped shallots in the wine until all the liquid has evaporated. Add the stock and continue to cook until the shallots are soft and the liquid sticky. Season with salt, pepper and a generous amount of cayenne, then leave it to cook a little.

Make a mayonnaise with the yolks, mustard and vinegar and slowly whisk in the oil. Once made, add the shallot mix and check the seasoning. The sauce should have a good kick and be a little sharp.

When you're ready to eat, cut the head into 2cm slices and then remove the string and cling film – they help to keep everything in place as you slice. Heat a tablespoon of vegetable oil and fry the slices until crispy on both sides. Serve with the mayonnaise and some roast vegetables.

Bolo de Caco with Pig's Liver and Onions

A classic dish in Madeira, bola de caco is a muffin-like bread containing sweet potato. It's traditionally cooked on a stone slab over a wood fire, but a small iron pan on the hob is fine. Once the bread is cooked, serve it filled with liver and onions. White sweet potatoes are best here, but you can use the orange kind.

Serves 8

Bolo de caco

1	sweet potato
8g	fresh yeast (or 4g dried)
300ml	lukewarm water
500g	bread flour, plus extra for dusting
1 tsp	salt

Liver and onions

4 tbsp	vegetable oil
4	large onions, peeled and sliced
400g	pig's liver
100g	smoked bacon
2	bay leaves
100ml	Madeira
250ml	chicken stock
1 tbsp	red wine vinegar
	salt and freshly ground black pepper

Preheat the over to 200°C/Fan 180°C/Gas 6. Bake the sweet potato for about an hour or until tender, then leave it to cool. Scoop out the flesh and mash it with a fork – you need about 150g. Dissolve the yeast in the water in a bowl, then add the flour, mashed sweet potato and salt.

Mix well, then knead the dough for 5–6 minutes. Depending on the moisture content of the potato you may need to add a little more water. Cover the bowl and leave the dough in a warm place to rise for an hour.

Knock the dough back, then divide it into 8 balls. Flatten these with a rolling pin so they are 8–10cm wide. Heat a dry frying pan dusted with flour, add a few of the balls of dough and cook them for 7–8 minutes. Flip them and cook on the other side for 5–6 minutes – they should look nicely charred. Leave them to cool on a rack.

For the liver and onions, heat 2 tablespoons of the oil in a frying pan and add the onions. Season them with salt and pepper, then cook until golden brown and soft. Remove them from the pan and set aside.

Put the liver and bacon through the coarse plate of a mincer or chop them by hand. Heat the rest of the oil in the pan and add the liver and bacon, bay leaves and seasoning. Brown over a high heat, then add the Madeira, stock and the cooked onions. Continue to cook until the liquid has reduced and has the consistency of a sauce. Finish by adding the red wine vinegar.

Split the rolls in half, fill them with the liver mixture and serve at once.

Pig's Liver with Orange and Oyster Sauce

Pig's liver has a strong flavour and can be a little bitter so this recipe balances that with the oyster sauce and fruit. Serve this with some steamed rice and tenderstem broccoli.

Serves 4

2	oranges
400g	pig's liver
	vegetable oil
3	garlic cloves, peeled
30g	fresh root ginger
4 tbsp	oyster sauce
4 tbsp	dry sherry
1 tbsp	dark soy sauce
2 tsp	cornflour
2	spring onions, chopped
	salt and freshly ground black pepper

Peel the oranges with a sharp knife, removing as much of the white pith as you can. Divide them into segments – hold each orange over a bowl to catch any juice – then set the juice and segments aside separately.

Cut the liver into strips of about 4cm wide and season them with salt and pepper. Heat 2 tablespoons of oil in a pan and fry the liver over a very high heat until it's browned all over but still pink inside. Remove the liver and set it aside.

Slice the garlic and cut the ginger into matchsticks. Add a little more oil to the pan and gently fry the garlic and ginger until soft.

Mix the oyster sauce, sherry, soy sauce and cornflour with any juice from segmenting the oranges. Turn up the heat under the frying pan, add the liver, then the cornflour mixture. Simmer for 3–4 minutes until the sauce has thickened and the liver is cooked through. Add the orange segments and spring onions and serve immediately.

Caillettes

These little pig's liver parcels are the French version of faggots and can be served hot or cold. I love having some in the fridge for a snack or a quick meal. Charcuteries in France always have them on offer and all swear by their own particular recipe.

Serves 4

200g	pig's liver
250g	pork fat
100g	pork shoulder
2	garlic cloves, peeled and chopped
120g	mixed herbs, such as chives, sage, parsley, chopped
2	shallots, peeled and chopped
160g	pig's caul
	salt and freshly ground black pepper

Mince the liver, pork fat and shoulder, then mix in the garlic, herbs and shallots. Season the mixture well. Preheat the oven to 200°C/Fan 180°C/Gas 6.

Rinse the caul and lay it out on the work surface. Divide the meat into 4 or 5 balls and place them on the caul. Wrap the meatballs individually in the caul, tearing it as you go, and place them in an ovenproof dish – they should fit tightly. Bake in the preheated oven for 30 minutes.

You can serve these hot or cold, as a main dish or a snack. I like them cold with some hot toasted or grilled bread, drizzled with olive oil.

Blood Pancake 'Papi Marcel'

My late father-in-law used to make this with chicken blood after killing a chicken or rooster for Sunday lunch. Chicken blood is hard to get unless you rear your own chickens, but you can make the pancakes with pig's blood which is available from most butchers. The pancake resembles black pudding in colour and consistency.

Serves 2–4

250ml	pig's blood
1 handful	coarse dry breadcrumbs from a baguette
2 tbsp	olive oil
2	garlic cloves, peeled and finely chopped
2 tbsp	chopped flatleaf parsley
	salt and freshly ground black pepper

Mix the blood with the breadcrumbs in a bowl. Heat the oil in a frying pan and add the garlic, then when it starts to colour, add the blood and crumb mixture. Season with salt and pepper.

Cook this like a thick pancake, flipping it over to cook the other side. Sprinkle the pancake with parsley and serve it hot or cold, with a cup of coffee or a glass of red wine!

Stuffed Pig's Head with Andouillette

*Ask your butcher to bone the pig's head from the back, keeping it
in one piece with the ears attached. I must admit that this recipe
does need quite a bit of work, but it's perfectly achievable at
home and does make a really spectacular dish. Serve it hot with
Madeira sauce or cold with pickles and mustard. Once cooked,
the head keeps for about a week.*

Makes 12 big slices

500g	pork belly, diced
250g	lardo (cured pork fat), diced
150g	smoked bacon, diced
	sel rose (pink curing salt)
pinch	grated nutmeg
pinch	4-spice mix
	splash of brandy
1	whole pig's head, boned and with ears intact
4	andouillette sausages
1 tbsp	butter
6	shallots, peeled and finely chopped
1	calf's foot, split
4	onions, peeled
2	carrots, peeled
2	celery sticks
1 tsp	whole black peppercorns
	salt and freshly ground pepper

Madeira sauce

80g	butter
6	shallots, peeled and sliced
200ml	Madeira

Put the pork belly, lardo and smoked bacon in a bowl. Season the meat with salt, curing salt (check the packet instructions for the exact quantity needed), nutmeg, 4-spice and a splash of brandy, then cover and leave everything to marinate for 2 hours.

Clean and scrape the boned pig's head and singe off any hairs with a blowtorch. Cut each of the sausages into 6 pieces.

Melt the butter in a frying pan and cook the shallots until soft. Remove the pan from the heat and leave the shallots to cool.

Once the pork belly mixture has marinated, put it through a small mincing plate, then beat in the cooled shallots. Make a small patty of the meat mixture, wrap it in buttered foil and cook it in a medium oven for 10 minutes. Taste and adjust the seasoning to taste.

Using a trussing needle and butcher's string, stitch up the eyes and mouth of the head. This will stop the stuffing from escaping during cooking. Place the head in a bowl with the snout down so the back of the head is towards you and you can see inside. Season the inside of the head, then pack a little of the minced meat mixture into the snout. Place a ring of andouillette into the mince and then pack with some more mince. Keep adding mince and sausage in a regular pattern, filling all the gaps once occupied by bone to reshape the head. Eventually you will have replaced all the bone with mince and andouillette. Leave a gap about 3cm from the top and stitch up the back of the head with butcher's string.

Cut strips of muslin cloth and wrap up the head tightly, like a mummy! This will keep everything in place and prevent the head splitting open while cooking.

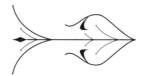

Place the head in a large saucepan of cold water and add the calf's foot and vegetables. Season with salt and black peppercorns. Bring the water to the boil, then reduce the heat and simmer for about 4½ hours. The head must stay submerged in the liquid and needs to simmer very gently or it is likely to burst.

To check if the head is cooked, insert a thin needle or skewer. It should easily pass into the meat and the tip should be hot. Remove the pan from the heat but leave the head in the pan of liquid to cool.

When the head is cool, very gently remove it from the liquid, place it on a tray and leave it in the fridge overnight to set. Pass the stock through a sieve and reserve the liquid.

The next day, carefully remove the muslin cloth and snip the strings tying the eyes, mouth and back of the head together and remove them. To serve the head cold, place it upright on a serving dish and brush all over with a little of the cooking liquid to give it a shine.

To serve hot, preheat the oven to 180°C/Fan 160°C/Gas 4 and place the head in an ovenproof dish with 500ml of the cooking liquid. Loosely cover with buttered foil so the foil is not in contact with the skin. Put the head in the oven for about 1½ hours to reheat gently. Don't be tempted to turn the heat up or the skin will split.

Meanwhile, make the Madeira sauce. Melt a tablespoon of the butter in a frying pan and sweat the shallots until they're soft and golden brown. Add the Madeira and cook to reduce it by three-quarters before adding 1 litre of the reserved cooking liquid. Bring to the boil and reduce again by a half. Pass the sauce through a fine sieve and whisk in the remaining butter to make a glossy sauce.

Remove the foil from the head for the last 10 minutes of the cooking time. Brush the head all over with some of the sauce to give it a shiny sticky glaze. Carve the head at the table and serve it with the sauce, some boiled potatoes and green beans or peas.

LE

BETAIL

LE BETAIL: *cattle – cows and calves*

With any meat from the cow, the larger and older the animal, the stronger the taste and the longer it needs to be cooked. Ox heart, for example, needs to be cooked long and slow until it's meltingly tender. Ox kidneys have a strong flavour that works beautifully in small quantities in dishes such as steak and kidney pudding or pie, but most people find them too powerful on their own.

By the way, you may wonder why the term 'ox' is used for some parts of the animal. The explanation seems to go way back in time, with ox referring to what were considered the less choice cuts, such as cheeks and tail.

The meat from young calves, known as veal, is much milder. Veal kidneys are perfect for quick sautéeing, and calf's liver is the sweetest, and many say the best, of all livers, responding well to brief cooking. Calf's brains are some of the loveliest of all offal, with a wonderful creamy texture, and they are very easy to prepare, as are calf sweetbreads (pancreas and thymus glands). There were health and safety concerns about brains after the BSE outbreak in the 1980s, but brains are now safe to eat as long as they come from animals under 12 months old. Your butcher will advise you.

Many people want food that is easy to prepare, simple to cook and easy to eat. They feel challenged by offal and avoid it. Tripe, for instance, was once a commonplace food, sold in every butchers' shop at a time when every part of an animal had to be used. You still see it in ethnic markets in the UK, more in other parts of Europe, and it is slowly coming back into fashion. Cooks are now becoming braver, willing to explore different tastes and textures. Supermarkets are stocking oxtail and bone marrow, but you may have to look further afield for some of the more unusual items such as beef tendons. Talk to your local butcher and find out what they can order, or check online for suppliers. You may be pleasantly surprised at what is on offer.

Bone Marrow Croquettes

Bone marrow is extremely nutritious as well as being very good to eat. It had fallen out of favour but has seen a big surge in popularity in recent years so is much easier to get. I love these croquettes as a snack with a drink, or they make an excellent garnish to serve with roast beef.

Makes 16 croquettes

600g	trimmed bone marrow, cut into long pieces
1 sprig	thyme
2	bay leaves
120g	butter
400g	white mushrooms, very finely chopped
2	shallots, peeled and chopped
2 tbsp	chopped flatleaf parsley
300ml	milk
80g	flour, plus extra for dusting
	Dijon mustard
2	eggs, beaten
600g	fine breadcrumbs
	vegetable oil, for deep-frying
	salt and freshly ground black pepper

Put the pieces of bone marrow in a bowl of cold water and leave them to soak for a couple of hours. Transfer them to a saucepan of fresh water and add the thyme and bay. Bring the water to a simmer and cook the marrow for 5 minutes. Refresh it in iced water, then drain. Cut the marrow into 16 x 1cm cubes, then roughly chop the rest.

Melt 40g of the butter in a frying pan. Add the mushrooms and shallots and cook until the pan is dry. Lightly season with salt and pepper and add the parsley, then set aside.

Bring the milk to the boil. Melt the remaining butter in a separate pan, then add the 80g of flour and stir to make a roux. Gradually whisk in the milk to make a béchamel and cook for 10 minutes. Set the sauce aside to cool, then fold in the mushrooms and shallots and the chopped bone marrow. Keep the cubes for later.

Check the seasoning, then spoon or pipe the mixture into silicone moulds approximately 3cm deep, the shape of your choice. This should fill about 16.

Push a marrow cube into each one, followed by a dab of Dijon mustard, then cover with more of the mix. Place the croquettes in the freezer until hard, then press them out of the moulds.

Roll the croquettes in flour, then beaten egg and finally breadcrumbs. Half-fill a large saucepan or a deep-fat fryer with oil and heat the oil to 180°C. Fry the croquettes a few at a time until crisp and hot inside. Serve with beetroot ketchup (see page 249).

Bone Marrow and Pea Toast

This is a lovely way of serving bone marrow and makes a very pretty dish; it's an excellent starter or light lunch.

Serves 4

200g	shelled peas, fresh or frozen
380g	veal bone marrow
4	large slices of country-style sourdough bread
	olive oil
2	garlic cloves, peeled and finely crushed
1 sprig	fresh mint, chopped
2	spring onions, thinly sliced
	squeeze of lemon juice
	pea shoots, to garnish
	sea salt and freshly ground black pepper

Blanch the peas in salted, boiling water until cooked, then refresh them in iced water. Drain the peas when cold and set them aside.

Cut the bone marrow into 1cm slices, keeping the trimmings and offcuts separate, and set aside.

Brush the slices of bread with a little olive oil and grill them until slightly charred. Set them aside to keep warm.

Place a frying pan over a low heat, add the offcuts of bone marrow and let them melt and render their fat. Turn up the heat and place the slices of bone marrow in the pan.

Cook them for about 30 seconds on each side, until just translucent – don't overcook them. Carefully take the marrow slices out of the pan and place them in a warm dish.

Add the garlic and peas to the pan and squash them with the back of a fork. Once the peas are hot, add a little chopped mint, the spring onions and a squeeze of lemon juice.

Spread the pea mixture on the toast and top with the bone marrow slices. Season with salt and pepper, garnish with pea shoots and serve at once.

Bone Marrow Butter

This butter is delicious on toast or warm bread but you can't cook with it, as it burns quickly. Ask your butcher just to crack the bones, not split them, so the marrow can ooze out. And go for middle-section marrow bones as they contain more marrow. If you like, you can add extra oomph by using flavoured salt, such as smoked sea salt or chilli salt.

Makes about 450g

3kg	veal marrow bones, cracked
4 tsp	Maldon sea salt

Preheat the oven to 220°C/Fan 200°C/Gas 7. Place the bones in a large roasting tin and place them in a hot oven for 15 minutes.

Once the bones start to colour, reduce the heat to 110°C/Fan 90°C/Gas ¼ and leave them in the oven for another 2 hours. By then all the marrow will have melted and the bones will be empty. Remove the tin from the oven and carefully pour the liquid into a bowl. Keep the bones to use in a stock.

Line a sieve with a piece of muslin and pass the melted marrow through this to ensure there aren't any fragments of bone remaining. While the marrow is still hot, add the salt and mix well.

Leave the marrow to cool. Once it starts to change colour and solidify, whisk well, ideally over a bowl of iced water, until it emulsifies and turns opaque. It's ready when it looks like butter. Check the seasoning and add a little more salt if needed.

The butter can now be used or covered and stored in a container in the fridge for up to 10 days. Be sure to remove it from the fridge and bring it back to room temperature before serving.

Roast Marrow Bones and Crispy Ox Tongue

The deep-fried tongue provides a good contrast to the unctuous bone marrow and this makes a perfect starter. Ask your butcher to split the bones for you.

Serves 4

4	veal marrow bones, about 12–14cm long, split in half lengthways
320g	cooked ox tongue
3 tbsp	potato flour
	vegetable oil, for deep-frying
2	large shallots, peeled and cut into thin rings
3 sprigs	flatleaf parsley
2	firm mushrooms, thinly sliced
	sherry vinegar
	salt and freshly ground black pepper

Preheat the oven to 200°C/Fan 180°C/Gas 6. Place the bones, cut-side up, in a large roasting tin and lightly season them with salt and pepper. Roast them in the oven for 15–20 minutes, depending on the thickness of the bone marrow. The marrow should be hot with a little colour.

Cut the tongue into 1cm cubes and dust them in potato flour. Half-fill a large saucepan or a deep-fat fryer with vegetable oil and heat to 180°C. Deep-fry the ox tongue cubes in batches for 1 minute until crisp, then drain on kitchen paper.

To serve, place cubes of deep-fried tongue along the marrow bones and garnish with raw shallot rings, parsley leaves and slices of mushroom. Finish with a few drops of sherry vinegar.

Roast Marrow Bones and Ceps

This is quite a rich dish and makes a nice starter or a light main course. If ceps aren't in season, use any other mushrooms. Ask your butcher to split the bones for you.

Serves 4

4	veal marrow bones (about 12–14cm long), split in half lengthways
1 tbsp	vegetable oil
200g	cep mushrooms, cleaned and diced
2	shallots, peeled and finely chopped
2	garlic cloves, peeled and finely chopped
3 tbsp	chopped flatleaf parsley
4 slices	white bread, crusts removed and cut into cubes
	salt and freshly ground black pepper

Preheat the oven to 200°C/Fan 180°C/Gas 6. Season the marrow bones with salt and pepper.

Place the bones in a large roasting tin, cut-side down, and place them in the preheated oven.

Meanwhile, heat the oil in a frying pan and add the diced mushrooms. Sauté them over a high heat, then season with salt and pepper. Add the chopped shallots and continue to cook for 2 minutes before adding the chopped garlic. Cook for a further minute, then remove the pan from the heat and add the parsley.

When the marrow has been in the oven for 10 minutes turn the bones over and sprinkle the cubes of bread on top of the bones. Put the roasting tin back in the oven for another 10 minutes.

Serve the bones with the garlicky mushrooms, the croutons and any melted marrow fat.

Grilled Veal Kidneys with Warm Mustard Mayonnaise

This is a quick and simple recipe but tastes great. You will have more mayonnaise than you need, but you can chill any that's left and keep it in the fridge for a couple of weeks to use with cold meat, sandwiches or anything else you fancy.

Serves 2

1	veal kidney, fat removed
1 tbsp	vegetable oil
	salt and freshly ground black pepper

Warm mustard mayonnaise

120ml	milk
½	garlic clove, peeled and very finely chopped
1	bay leaf
1 sprig	thyme
2 tsp	Dijon mustard
2 tsp	English mustard
2 tsp	wholegrain mustard
1 tbsp	white wine vinegar
80ml	vegetable oil

Take the kidney and using the point of a knife, remove the sinew and any fat remaining in the core. Open out the kidney but keep it in one piece, with all the little knobs still attached.

To make the mustard mayonnaise, put the milk in a pan with the garlic, bay leaf, thyme and a pinch of salt. Bring it to the boil, then leave it to cool. When the milk is tepid, remove the bay leaf and thyme, then add the mustards and vinegar. Using a stick blender at full speed, mix well, then slowly add the oil to make the mayonnaise.

Season the kidney with salt and pepper, drizzle with a little vegetable oil and then cook it on a barbecue or a very hot griddle pan. For pink meat, cook for 5 minutes on each side. Leave the kidney to rest in a warm place for 3 or 4 minutes. Discard any juices that run.

Serve the kidney with the warm mayo, chips and a side salad.

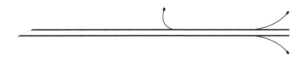

Whole Roast Veal Kidney with Gingerbread Crumb

I like to give an Asian twist to a classic roast kidney by using flavours such as ginger, coriander and sesame. The kidney is encased in gingery crumbs, ideally from a French pain d'épices or, failing that, an English ginger cake. Pain d'épices is made with rye flour and flavoured with honey and spices. They do a fantastic version in the Alsace area of France but each region is fiercely protective of their own recipe and claims it is the best!

Serves 2

1	veal kidney in its fat
1	shallot, peeled and sliced
2	garlic cloves, peeled and crushed
1 tbsp	chopped fresh root ginger
4 tbsp	red wine vinegar
260ml	veal stock
4 tbsp	crumbs from a pain d'épices (or ginger cake)
3 tbsp	chopped fresh coriander
1 tbsp	roasted sesame oil
	salt and freshly ground black pepper

The kidney must be completely encased in its fat – this is very important. Carefully trim some of the fat, leaving a thickness of 1cm all around the kidney. Preheat the oven to 200°C/Fan 180°C/Gas 6.

Season the kidney well with salt and pepper and place it in a flameproof casserole dish over a high heat. Colour it on all sides – no extra fat needed – then place it in the preheated oven for 10 minutes. Add the shallot, garlic and ginger, turn the oven down to 180°C/Fan 160°C/Gas 4 and continue to roast for another 30 minutes. Leave the oven on.

Remove the kidney, leaving the shallots and other flavourings in the pan, and allow to rest in a warm place. Put the pan back on the hob and deglaze it with the vinegar, then add the stock.

Simmer until the mixture has the consistency of a light sauce, then pass it through a fine sieve. Leave it to settle, then carefully spoon off the fat.

Roll the kidney in the gingerbread crumbs, then put it back in oven for 10 minutes to reheat. The kidney should still be pink, but if you prefer it less rare, leave it for 15 minutes.

Meanwhile, bring the sauce to the boil and add the chopped coriander and sesame oil.

To serve, slice the kidney and serve with the sauce, perhaps some sautéed spinach and a glass of Spätlese Riesling.

Veal Sweetbread Pie

This was a popular dish in the early days of Le Gavroche and I still love it. Your butcher should be able to order veal sweetbreads for you and there are also a number of online suppliers, selling rose veal sweetbreads. This dish is best with morel mushrooms when you can get them; otherwise use whatever you can find.

Serves 4

600–800g	veal sweetbreads
2 tbsp	white wine vinegar
	flour, for dusting
2 tbsp	vegetable oil
2 tbsp	butter
220g	fresh morel mushrooms
50ml	brandy
1 litre	veal stock, boiled to reduce to 200ml
150ml	double cream
200g	puff pastry
1	egg, beaten
	salt and freshly ground black pepper

Place the sweetbreads in a bowl of cold water and leave them to soak for an hour. Drain, then put the sweetbreads in a saucepan, cover with cold water and add salt and the vinegar. Bring to the boil, then take the pan off the heat and leave the sweetbreads to cool.

When the sweetbreads are cool enough to handle, peel off the membrane and any gristle. Break the sweetbreads up into large nuggets and dredge them in seasoned flour.

Heat the oil and butter in a frying pan. Add the sweetbreads and fry them until golden, then transfer them to a pie dish. Add the mushrooms to the pan and fry until lightly cooked, then add them to the pie dish.

Deglaze the pan with the brandy, scraping up any sticky bits, then add the stock and cream. Simmer to make a light sauce, then season with salt and pepper. Pour the sauce over the pie filling and set aside to cool. Preheat the oven to 180°C/Fan 160°C/Gas 4.

When the filling is cool, roll out the puff pastry and place it over the pie. Trim the edges and cut a hole in the centre for the steam to escape. Brush the pie with beaten egg and decorate with the pastry trimmings if you like. Bake in the preheated oven for 30 minutes, then serve hot with some lightly steamed asparagus.

Sweetbread and Black Pudding Dartois

A dartois is a kind of puff pastry tart made in an oblong shape, with the top crust slashed at regular intervals. The filling can be sweet or savoury – in this version I use a flavoursome mixture of sweetbreads and black pudding, bound together with a chicken breast mousse.

Serves 4

1	chicken supreme, skinned and trimmed of sinew
1	egg white
200ml	double cream
300g	veal sweetbreads
	white wine vinegar
	flour, for dusting
100g	butter
120g	black pudding
350g	puff pastry
1	egg, beaten
	sea salt

Chop the chicken roughly and put it in a blender with the egg white. Blitz until smooth and then, with the blender running, slowly add the double cream. Season with salt, then chill the mousse in the fridge.

Rinse the sweetbreads in cold water and place them in a saucepan. Cover with cold water, season with salt and add a splash of white wine vinegar. Bring to a gentle simmer and cook for about 5 minutes. Leave them to cool in the liquid.

When the sweetbreads are cool enough to handle, gently peel off the outer membrane and trim away any fatty sinew. Cut the sweetbreads into bite-sized nuggets and dust them in seasoned flour. Melt the butter in a frying pan and once it is hot, add the sweetbreads and brown them all over. Set them aside to cool. Cut the black pudding into similar-sized pieces and mix them with the chicken mousse and the sweetbreads. Season with salt and pepper.

Roll the puff pastry into a square about 30cm by 30cm and about 3mm thick. Cut off the top 14cm so you have 2 pieces of pastry, one slightly larger than the other.

Fold the larger piece along the longest side. Starting about 3cm from one end, make cuts in the folded edge about 1cm apart, cutting about two-thirds into the pastry. Open out the piece – it should have cuts through the middle with a border all around.

Brush around the edges of the remaining piece of pastry with beaten egg and place it on a baking sheet lined with greaseproof paper. Spoon the sweetbread mixture along the centre of the pastry. Place the larger piece of pastry on top and press down all the edges firmly. Trim the edges and brush the pastry with beaten egg. Chill for 30 minutes. Preheat the oven to 200°C/Fan 180°C/Gas 6. Bake the dartois for about 35 minutes until golden brown. Delicious!

Terrine of Sweetbreads and Lobster

This is an extravagant, luxurious dish – something to make when you have plenty of time and you want a real treat to serve up for special guests. There is quite a bit to do, but nothing tricky, and the result is spectacular. Great served hot or cold with beurre blanc (page 252).

Serves 12

500g	veal sweetbreads
2 tbsp	white wine vinegar
1	cooked lobster (about 400g)
250ml	dry white wine
1 tsp	tomato paste
400ml	double cream
200g	salmon, skin and bones removed
1	egg white
1 tbsp	vegetable oil
80g	butter
2	shallots, peeled and diced
1	carrot, peeled and diced
180g	celeriac, peeled and diced
1 sprig	rosemary, leaves finely chopped
20ml	brandy
	grated zest of 1 lemon
120g	large spinach leaves
	salt and freshly ground black pepper

Rinse the sweetbreads in cold water. Put them in a saucepan, cover them with cold water and add the white wine vinegar and a generous pinch of salt. Bring to the boil, then turn the heat down to a gentle simmer and cook for 2 minutes. Take the pan off the heat and set aside.

When the sweetbreads are cool enough to handle, gently peel off the outer membrane and trim away any fatty sinew, then split them into nuggets. Put the sweetbreads on kitchen paper to drain and leave them in the fridge.

Crack open the lobster and cut the meat into nuggets about the same size as the sweetbreads. Leave them in the fridge until needed.

Break down the lobster shell with a rolling pin and put it in a pan with the wine and tomato paste. Bring to the boil then add 200ml of the cream and simmer for 10 minutes. Pass the mixture through a sieve, then set aside.

Blitz the salmon with the egg white until smooth, then add the remaining cream. Blitz for 30 seconds – no more, or the mixture may split. Tip the mixture into a bowl and put it in the fridge.

Heat the oil and 40g of the butter in a large pan until foaming. Add the sweetbreads and fry them until golden, then add the shallots, carrot and celeriac and continue to cook over a low heat for about 5 minutes. Season well with a generous amount of pepper and the chopped rosemary, then remove the sweetbreads and vegetables from the pan and set them aside.

Deglaze the pan with the brandy, then add the lobster and lemon zest. Take the pan off the heat.

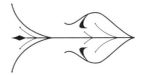

Bring a pan of salted water to the boil, add the spinach leaves and blanch them briefly. Drain and refresh the leaves in iced water. Carefully drain the leaves again and lay them out flat on a clean tea towel.

Grease a loaf tin with the remaining butter and line it with the spinach, leaving plenty overhanging the sides for covering the terrine later. Preheat the oven to 180°/Fan 160°C/Gas 4.

Mix the sweetbreads, cream mixture, salmon and lobster together with a spatula and then press it all into the terrine. Fold over the spinach leaves and cover with well-buttered foil. Place the terrine in a roasting tin and add hot water to come 3cm up the sides of the loaf tin. Bake in the preheated oven for 90 minutes.

Leave the terrine to cool, then place it in the fridge to chill for 12 hours. Delicious as it is but you can also serve it hot. Slice and put the slices on greaseproof paper in a steamer to warm through. Serve with beurre blanc (see page 252).

Spiced Ox Heart Kebabs

Ox heart is a healthy meat – low in fat and rich in protein – and very good to eat. The heart is a hard-working organ so it's best either cooked fast and briefly or long and slowly. Anything in between can leave it rather tough. This is a speedy recipe that makes a great barbecue snack.

Serves 4

500g	ox heart	1 tbsp	black peppercorns
2 tbsp	cumin seeds	2	garlic cloves, peeled
2 tbsp	coriander seeds	1	small shallot, peeled
2 tbsp	dry chilli flakes	2 tbsp	olive oil
1 tbsp	coarse sea salt	4 tbsp	red wine vinegar

Trim the heart to remove any sinew and silvery skin. Cut the meat into strips of about 1.5cm thick by 14cm long.

Toast the cumin and coriander seeds in a dry pan to release the aromas. Put them into a spice grinder or mortar, add the chilli flakes, coarse salt and peppercorns, then grind to a coarse powder. Tip the spice mixture into a bowl and mix in the garlic, shallot, oil and vinegar to make a paste.

Massage this paste into the strips of meat. Put them on a plate, cover with cling film and refrigerate for 24 hours.

When you're ready to cook, thread the strips of meat on to skewers and cook them on a barbecue or on a griddle pan. They need about 2 minutes on each side over a high heat for medium-rare meat.

Calf's Brain and Black Pudding Wellington

A take on beef wellington, this is not an everyday dish, I admit, but it is quite simply divine. I dare you to try it! Your butcher should be able to order veal brains for you or try online suppliers. Serve with a red wine sauce (page 255).

Serves 4

1	calf's brain
2 tbsp	white wine vinegar
260g	black pudding
300g	puff pastry
	flour, for dusting
1	egg, beaten
	salt

Pancakes

100ml	milk
1	small egg
40g	flour
1 tsp	oil
pinch	salt
	butter, for frying

Mushroom duxelle

10g	butter
1	large shallot, peeled and finely chopped
1	garlic clove, peeled and finely chopped
250g	white mushrooms, trimmed, wiped clean and chopped
1 sprig	thyme, leaves picked
	juice of ½ lemon
100ml	double cream
2 tbsp	chopped flatleaf parsley
	salt and freshly ground black pepper

First make the pancake batter. Whisk the milk and egg in a bowl, then whisk in the flour, oil and a pinch of salt to make a smooth batter. Grease a non-stick frying pan with a little butter and cook 3 or 4 very thin pancakes. You will have more batter than you need, but it's good to have some spare just in case. Set the pancakes aside to cool.

For the duxelle, heat the butter in a pan, add the finely chopped shallot and garlic and cook until tender. Add the mushrooms and continue to cook until the pan is dry. Add the thyme leaves, lemon juice and cream, season with salt and pepper and continue to cook until the mixture is thick. Remove the pan from the heat and leave to cool completely, then mix in the parsley.

Place the brain in a pan, cover with cold water and add the vinegar. Season with salt, bring the water to a gentle simmer for 10 minutes, then remove the pan from the heat and leave the brain to cool. Carefully remove the brain from the water, then peel off any dark membrane. Put the brain in the fridge to chill. Cut the black pudding into slices 2cm thick.

Roll out the puff pastry on a floured work surface to make a rectangle 3mm thick and put it in the fridge to keep cool. Preheat the oven to 200°C/Fan 180°C/Gas 6.

Place a row of 3 pancakes on your work surface with the edges overlapping. Trim to make a rectangle measuring about 20 x 14cm. Spread the mushroom mixture over the pancakes, then add a row of black pudding slices on one half of the pancake rectangle. Place the brain on top of the black pudding, then fold the rest of the pancake over to cover neatly.

Gently place this on to one half of the puff pastry. Brush the edges of the pastry with beaten egg, fold the other half over to encase the filling and seal the edges. Trim off any excess pastry and brush the wellington with beaten egg. Decorate with pastry trimmings if you like.

Cook the wellington in the preheated oven for 25 minutes. Allow it to cool slightly, then slice and serve with a red wine sauce (see page 255).

Calf's Liver Loaf

This is an adaptation of an Escoffier classic and it's a lovely winter warmer; good served with some root vegetables.

Serves 8

1 tbsp	butter, plus extra for greasing
2	onions, peeled and very finely chopped
800g	calf's liver, thinly sliced
200g	white bread
200ml	milk
300ml	double cream
2	eggs, beaten
	grated nutmeg
	salt and freshly ground black pepper

Mushroom sauce

1 tbsp	butter
125g	white button mushrooms, cleaned and roughly chopped
2	garlic cloves, peeled and roughly chopped
1	shallot, peeled and roughly chopped
100ml	Madeira
200ml	single cream

Melt the butter in a frying pan and sweat the onions until cooked, but don't allow them to brown. Set them aside to cool.

Trim the liver of any sinew, then mince it finely. Put the bread in a bowl, add the milk and cream and leave until completely softened. Put the onions, liver and bread in a bowl and beat with a hand beater. Add the eggs, season with a grating of nutmeg and salt and pepper, then mix well.

Preheat the oven to 180°C/Fan 160°C/Gas 4. Butter a loaf tin and pour in the mixture. Cover with foil and then place the tin a roasting tray. Add hot water to come halfway up the sides of the loaf tin. Cook for 2 hours until the loaf feels firm to the touch and a skewer comes out clean. Leave the loaf to rest for 10–15 minutes before tipping it out.

To make the sauce, melt the butter in a saucepan and sweat the mushrooms, garlic and shallot until cooked but not coloured. Add the Madeira and boil until the pan is almost dry, then add the cream and seasoning. Simmer for 5 minutes, then pour everything into a blender and blitz until smooth.

Slice the loaf and serve it with the sauce and some root vegetables.

Calf's Liver and Bacon

One of the most familiar and best loved of all offal dishes, this is quick to prepare and is always delicious – as long as you don't overcook the liver!

Serves 6

	vegetable oil
4	sweet onions, thinly sliced
50ml	white wine
250ml	veal stock
1 tbsp	sherry vinegar
6	thin slices of calf's liver (about 160g each)
12	slices dry-cured streaky bacon
	salt and freshly ground black pepper

Heat a tablespoon of oil in a frying pan over a medium heat. Add the sliced onions and cook them gently for 10–15 minutes until they are soft and caramelised. Season with salt and pepper.

Add the white wine to the onions, bring to the boil, reduce by half then add the veal stock and the sherry vinegar. Bring back to the boil, then turn the heat down and simmer gently for 10 minutes.

Meanwhile, preheat the oven to 200°C/Fan 180°C/Gas 6. Heat a griddle pan on the hob. Season the liver and brush it with oil on both sides, then cook it on the griddle just long enough to mark it. Transfer the liver to an ovenproof tray and put it in the oven. Cook it for 2–3 minutes for pink meat or a little longer for medium. Grill the bacon until crispy and keep it warm.

Serve the liver with the sweet onion gravy and the crispy bacon. Creamy mash or a potato gratin are ideal accompaniments.

Calf Brains with Capers

Some people do feel a bit squeamish about brains, but they are an excellent food and they have a lovely creamy texture and good flavour. This is the classic way of serving brains in France.

Serves 4

6	calf brains
	white wine vinegar
	plain flour, for dusting
2 tbsp	vegetable oil
125g	salted butter
	juice and zest of 1 lemon
2 tbsp	fine capers
3 tbsp	roughly chopped flatleaf parsley
	salt and freshly ground black pepper

Rinse the brains in cold water for 10 minutes to remove any excess blood. Place them in a saucepan, cover with cold water and season with salt and a splash of vinegar. Bring the water to a simmer and blanch the brains for 4 minutes. Remove them from the pan, refresh them in a bowl of iced water, then drain well.

Trim any sinew and fat from the brains and cut each one in half. Season the flour with salt and pepper and lightly dust each piece of brain with flour. Heat a pan with a little oil and add a tablespoon of the butter. When it starts to foam, add the brains and cook them over a medium heat until they are golden brown and crispy all over. Remove the brains from the pan and keep them warm.

Add the remaining butter to the pan and cook until it's nut brown. Add the lemon juice and zest – the butter will foam up at this point – and then stir in the capers and parsley.

Serve the brains with boiled potatoes and spinach and pour the caper and parsley butter over them.

Tongue in Beer with Sauerkraut

This is a really hearty dish from the Alsace region. It's best served with boiled potatoes and a glass of beer.

Serves 8

1	salted ox tongue
1	fresh calf's tongue
2	330ml bottles of white beer or lager
6	onions, peeled
4	carrots, peeled
1	garlic bulb, split into cloves
1	bouquet garni
1	small savoy cabbage, cut into 8 wedges
1 tbsp	butter
750g	cooked sauerkraut
250ml	chicken stock
	salt and freshly ground black pepper

Rinse the ox tongue well in several changes of cold water. Place it in a large saucepan, cover it with water and bring the water to a simmer. Drain, then refill the pan with cold water, return it to the heat and bring the water back to a simmer. Check the water and if it is still very salty, discard it and repeat the process once more.

If the water is not too salty, add the calf's tongue to the pan, together with 1 bottle of beer, 4 of the onions (left whole), the carrots, garlic cloves and the bouquet garni. Bring to a simmer, skim and continue to simmer gently for about 2 hours or until the tongues are tender when pierced with a needle. Leave them to cool in the liquid.

Once the tongues are cool enough to handle, remove them from the pan. Peel off the outer skin and trim off any sinew around the roots. Set the tongues aside with the whole cooked onions and carrots. Pass the cooking liquid through a sieve and discard the garlic and bouquet garni. Pour the strained liquid back into the pan, and add the wedges of cabbage. Cover the pan and simmer the cabbage gently for 20 minutes until cooked through.

Thinly slice the remaining 2 onions. Heat the butter in a separate saucepan and gently sweat the sliced onions – don't allow them to colour. Add the cooked sauerkraut, the second bottle of beer and the chicken stock to the pan, then season and cook for 20 minutes over a low heat. Set the pan of sauerkraut aside and keep it warm.

Put the tongues back in the large pan with the cabbage. Slice the carrots and cut the cooked onions into wedges and add them all to the pan. Reheat gently.

When everything is hot, remove the tongues and slice them. Serve the sauerkraut in deep bowls with some of the cooking liquid and top with slices of ox and veal tongue and vegetables. Serve with some grain mustard and horseradish sauce on the side.

Calf's Tongue with Beans and Ceps

The tarbais bean is generally thought to be the prince of pulses, with a lovely flavour and thinner skin than most beans. Tarbais beans are expensive though and hard to find outside France so you can use haricot beans instead for this dish. If ceps are out of season or unavailable, use chestnut or portobello mushrooms.

Serves 8

1	fresh calf's tongue
1	onion, whole
1	celery stick
1	carrot, whole
1	bouquet garni
200g	dried tarbais or haricot beans, soaked overnight
2–3 tbsp	vegetable oil
2	shallots, finely chopped
250g	ceps, diced
500ml	chicken stock
100ml	double cream
	salt and freshly ground black pepper

Rinse the tongue and place it in a pan of cold water. Bring the water to the boil and skim before adding the onion, celery, carrot and bouquet garni. Season with salt, then simmer gently for 40 minutes. Then add the soaked, drained beans and cook for another hour or until the tongue is tender and the beans are done. You may need to top up the liquid with boiling water from time to time. Leave the tongue and beans to cool.

In a separate pan heat a tablespoon of oil and add the chopped shallots. Sweat the shallots gently for 4–5 minutes, but don't let them brown.

Turn up the heat slightly and add the mushrooms and sauté them together. Add the chicken stock and bring it to the boil, then reduce the liquid by half before adding the double cream. Bring to the boil and season well with salt and freshly ground pepper.

Take the cooled tongue out of the water and peel it, then cut it into slices. Drain the beans and discard the vegetables. Add the beans to the mushroom mixture, heat them through thoroughly and season as needed.

Heat some of the remaining oil in a non-stick pan and fry the slices of tongue on each side until crispy, adding more oil if needed. Spoon the beans and mushrooms into deep bowls along with the sauce and then top with slices of crispy tongue.

Tête de Veau Ravigote

Tête de veau, poached calf's head, is a diehard French classic, served in all the traditional Parisian brasseries with the deliciously herby, tangy sauce ravigote. It's not an elegant dish and not one for the faint-hearted, but it is beloved by many and a real treat on a cold winter day. The head is cooked in a blanc – a solution prepared with a tablespoon of flour per litre of water, plus salt and some vinegar or lemon juice.

Serves 12

1	calf's head with tongue, off the bone
2	lemons
	plain flour
	salt
1	onion, peeled and studded with 2 cloves
1	bouquet garni
	beef or veal suet

Sauce ravigote

100ml	vegetable oil
40ml	white wine vinegar
1 tbsp	fine capers
½ tbsp	chopped curly parsley
2 tbsp	snipped herbs (chives, tarragon, chervil)
1	white onion, peeled and finely chopped
	salt and freshly ground black pepper

Vegetables

4	carrots, peeled
2	leeks, trimmed
36	small new potatoes, scrubbed

Check the head for hair and burn off any that remain with a blowtorch. Put the head in a huge saucepan and cover it generously with cold water. Bring the water to the boil, then drain and rinse the pan clean. Rub the head with a cut lemon half and set it aside.

For the blanc, you need a tablespoon of flour and 5 grams of salt per litre of water. Assuming you will need about 6 litres of water to cover the head, put 6 tablespoons of flour and 30 grams of salt in a sieve. Pour the water through the sieve into the pan, then add 2 tablespoons of lemon juice, the onion and the bouquet garni. Bring the water to the boil, then leave it to cool slightly – it will look milky. Add the calf's head, then bring the water back to a gentle simmer and cover the pan with a layer of beef or veal suet. You can use a wet tea towel instead of suet if need be.

Cook the head for about 2 hours or until it's tender, then leave it until it's cool enough to handle. Drain the head, reserving some of the blanc for reheating the meat if necessary. Peel the tongue, then cut the tongue and head meat into big chunks of about 2–3cm thick – use everything, even the ears!

To make the sauce, mix all the ingredients together in a jug. Cook the vegetables separately in salted water, then cut the carrots and leeks into large pieces.

Serve the meat piping hot with the vegetables and the ravigote sauce. If necessary, reheat the meat and the vegetables in a little of the blanc.

Tête de Veau à la Tortue

A magnificent French classic, this calf's head dish is a favourite of Matthew Fort's family, and one I've made for them many times. The leftovers come home with me! It is a lot of work but very satisfying to cook and very well worth it. Despite the name, there's no turtle – the name comes from the herbs and seasoning used which are similar to those in turtle consommé. The cockscombs and cocks' kidneys (testicles) are vital, as they provide the gelatine and collagen that make the texture of this dish so special. As always with anything rich in collagen and gelatine, this must be served good and hot.

Serves at least 12

1	cooked calf's head with tongue (see page 167)	4 litres	veal stock
6	cooked cockscombs (see page 45)	2 tbsp	chopped rosemary
24	cooked cocks' kidneys (see page 45)	2 tbsp	chopped marjoram
360g	butter	2 tbsp	chopped basil
1	large onion, peeled and sliced	36	button mushrooms
2 tbsp	plain flour	24	small onions, peeled and blanched
2 tbsp	concentrated tomato paste	24	green olives in brine, pitted
300ml	Madeira	2	whole black truffles (about 80g), sliced
200ml	truffle juice		basil and marjoram leaves
			salt and freshly ground black pepper

The day before you want to serve this dish, cook the calf's head (see page 167), cockcombs (see page 45) and cocks' kidneys (see page 45) and keep them in the fridge until needed.

On the day, melt 2 tablespoons of the butter in a large saucepan and cook the sliced onion until brown, then add the flour and the tomato paste. Stir well and cook for a further 5 minutes, then add the Madeira to deglaze the pan. Mix well to avoid lumps, then add the truffle juice, veal stock and herbs. Simmer this stock for 45 minutes, then pass it through a fine sieve and set it aside.

Melt another tablespoon of butter in a large pan and sweat the button mushrooms and blanched onions for 10 minutes. Add the stock you prepared earlier and bring it to a simmer. Cut the veal head into large cubes, about 4cm, the combs into 2 or 3 pieces and leave the testicles whole. When the stock is simmering add all the meat to the pan and simmer for 30 minutes. Season well, then add the remaining butter to finish

Serve piping hot and garnished with the olives, sliced truffles and a few leaves of basil and marjoram. Boiled potatoes are an essential accompaniment.

Calf's Foot Salad

Again, this is all about texture – the textures of the different parts of the meat contrasting with the crisp vegetables. A fresh, Asian-style dressing completes the dish. Ask your butcher to split the calves' feet for you so you don't do yourself a mischief.

Serves 4

2	calves' feet, split
1	onion, peeled and roughly chopped
1	carrot, peeled and roughly chopped
1	celery stick, peeled and roughly chopped
1	bouquet garni
	salt

Salad

2	red onions, peeled and finely sliced
2 tbsp	rice vinegar
1	carrot, peeled
1	turnip, peeled
1	kohlrabi
	soy sauce
20g	fresh root ginger, finely minced
2 tbsp	chopped coriander
	olive oil
	salt and freshly ground black pepper

Wash the calves' feet well, burn off any hairs with a blowtorch. Put the feet in a large saucepan and cover them with cold water. Bring the water to the boil, skim and season with salt. Add the onion, carrot, celery and bouquet garni, turn down the heat and simmer gently for 2–2½ hours. At the end of the cooking time, the meat should be falling off the bones.

Remove the pan from the heat, drain the feet and leave them to cool. When the feet are cool, take all meat off the bones – including the skin and gelatinous bits – and cut it into thin strips. Put all the meat in a large bowl and set aside.

To make the salad, place the slices of red onion in the rice vinegar to soak – this removes any bitterness. Slice all the vegetables into thin strips or use a spiraliser to cut them into long 'spaghetti' and add them to the meat in the bowl. Drain the onions and add them to the bowl, reserving the vinegar for the dressing.

Mix the rice vinegar with a little soy sauce, minced ginger and the chopped coriander. Whisk in enough olive oil to form a dressing. Taste and adjust the seasoning. Pour the dressing over the salad, mix well and serve.

Spicy Calf's Foot and Chickpea Stew

For those who enjoy a calf's foot this one is a must – the flavours are really intense and there's lots of interesting texture. I suggest you don't bone the feet and just let everyone pick off the meat for themselves. Messy but nice.

Serves 4

2	calves' feet, split
2 tbsp	cumin seeds
1½ tbsp	paprika
4	garlic cloves, peeled and finely chopped
¼ tsp	crushed dried chilli flakes
100g	cracked wheat
250g	chickpeas, soaked overnight
80g	golden raisins
60g	pine nuts
1	lemon
	salt and freshly ground black pepper

Wash the calves' feet well, burn off any hairs with a blowtorch. Put the feet in a large saucepan and cover with 3.5 litres of cold water. Season with salt and pepper and bring the water to the boil. Skim the surface, then turn down the heat and simmer the feet for 50 minutes.

Toast the cumin seeds in a dry pan for a few minutes, then add the paprika and toast it lightly. Blend the spices to a powder, then add them to the pan with the feet after the initial 50 minutes cooking, together with the garlic, chilli, cracked wheat and the drained chickpeas. Bring the water back to a simmer and continue to cook for another 1½ hours.

At the end of the cooking time the feet should be tender and the chickpeas cooked. The broth should have thickened with the addition of the wheat, but if it seems too thin bring it to the boil and continue until it has reduced to a good thick consistency. Check and adjust the seasoning.

Blanch the raisins briefly in boiling water and toast the pine nuts in a dry pan until lightly golden. Sprinkle the raisins and pine nuts on top of the stew, add a squeeze of lemon and serve.

Pani Ca' Meusa

Sicilian spleen sandwiches – a cornbread bun filled with warm veal spleen and cheese, this is a Sicilian street food classic. What's not to like?

Serves 8–12

Cornbread buns

15g	yeast (or 7g dried)
275ml	lukewarm water
1 tbsp	olive oil
175g	polenta
375g	bread flour
12g	fine salt
10g	caster sugar

Filling

1kg	veal spleen
2 tbsp	coarse sea salt
1 sprig	rosemary
3	bay leaves
100g	lard
	caciocavallo cheese
	ricotta (optional)
	salt and freshly ground black pepper

First make the buns. Dissolve the yeast in 275ml of lukewarm water, add the oil and all the dry ingredients. Knead until you have a smooth, elastic dough, then put it in a bowl, cover and leave it to rise in a warm place.

When the dough has risen to twice its size, knock it back then divide it into 60–80g balls. Cover these and leave them to rise again. Preheat the oven to 220°C/Fan 200°C/Gas 7. Brush the buns with water and cook them in the hot oven for 10 minutes. Remove them and set aside.

Carefully trim the membrane off the spleen. Place the spleen in a large saucepan with the salt, rosemary and bay. Cover with cold water, bring to the boil, then simmer for 90 minutes. By this time, the spleen should be tender and soft enough for a knife to pierce easily.

Drain the spleen and leave it to cool, then cut it into slices 5mm thick. Melt the lard in a frying pan and add the slices of spleen to reheat. Season with a little salt and pepper.

Pile the warm spleen into the buns and add slices of caciocavallo cheese. If you want things even more rich and cheesy, add a good scoop of ricotta as well.

Potted Tongue with Mustard

Potted meats used to be very popular and they were an excellent method of preserving. The butter acted as a lid to protect the food. Ox tongue is perfect for this technique and is cheap to buy and highly nutritious. These little pots will keep for 10 days in the fridge and make an ideal starter or snack; the meat is great in sandwiches too. Ask your butchers if they can supply salted ox tongue or check online for suppliers.

Makes 12 small pots

1	salted ox tongue
1	onion, peeled and roughly chopped
2	celery sticks, roughly chopped
1	carrot, peeled and roughly chopped
1	bouquet garni
1 tsp	ground mace
1 tbsp	wholegrain mustard
150g	unsalted butter, softened, plus extra for sealing the pots
	freshly ground black pepper

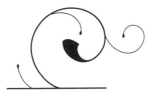

Rinse the tongue and place it in a saucepan of cold water. Bring the water to a simmer and then discard it. Refill the pan with fresh water and bring it back to a simmer. Skim well and add the vegetables and the bouquet garni. Cook the tongue gently for about 2 hours until tender. Leave it to cool in the liquid.

Once the tongue is cool, remove it from the liquid. Peel off the skin and trim any sinew around the root area. Chop the meat into small pieces by hand or in a food processor for a smoother texture.

Put the chopped tongue in a bowl and season with mace, mustard and some black pepper. Mix in the softened butter and beat well. Spoon the mixture into small ramekins or pots – or into one large dish if you prefer. Top with melted butter to seal, then put in the fridge to chill and set. Serve with toast.

Ox Tongue Fricassée

This is an Escoffier classic and is very rich and delicious. Traditionally the fricassée is served on slices of fried bread as I have suggested here.

Serves 6

1	fresh ox tongue
	plain flour, for dusting
	vegetable oil
60g	butter
2	white onions, peeled and sliced
4	Jerusalem artichokes, peeled and sliced
2	garlic cloves, peeled and very finely chopped
200ml	Madeira
200ml	veal stock
6 slices	rustic bread
1	raw truffle (30–40g), sliced into matchsticks
	salt and freshly ground black pepper

Wash the tongue in cold water. Place it in a pan with a generous amount of salt, cover with water and bring the water to the boil. Simmer the tongue for 2 hours or until it's tender. Leave the tongue to cool in the water, then peel off the skin and refrigerate it overnight.

Trim off any sinew around the root, then cut the tongue into small slices, about 5cm wide and 5mm thick. Dust them with seasoned flour. Heat a couple of tablespoons of oil in a frying pan and fry the slices of tongue until lightly coloured on both sides. You might need to do this in a couple of batches, setting each batch aside in a warm place.

When all the tongue is fried, discard the fat in the pan and add a tablespoon of the butter. Sweat the onions and Jerusalem artichokes until translucent and tender, then add the garlic and continue to cook for a further 2-3 minutes.

Pour in the Madeira and let it boil for 5 minutes, then add the stock and simmer for 2-3 minutes. Put the tongue back in the pan and add the remaining butter.

Meanwhile, fry the bread in vegetable oil until golden.

Season the fricassée with salt and pepper and finish with the slices of truffle. Serve on slices of fried bread.

Oxtail in Crépinette

In crépinette means wrapped in caul fat. These little oxtail parcels are then glazed in the oven and served with a sauce made of the reduced cooking liquid.

Serves 6

1 tbsp	butter
1 tbsp	vegetable oil
12–16	pieces of oxtail
2	onions, peeled
4	carrots, peeled
2	celery sticks, trimmed
1 bottle	red wine
250ml	port
1	bouquet garni
2	garlic cloves, peeled
75g	smoked bacon, chopped
1.5 litres	veal stock
	caul fat
	salt and freshly ground black pepper

Heat the butter and oil in a large saucepan. Season the oxtail pieces all over, then brown them in the pan. Do this in batches, setting each batch aside as it is browned.

Once all the oxtail has been browned, add the whole onions, carrots and celery sticks to the pan and allow them to colour slightly before adding the wine, port, bouquet garni and garlic cloves. Bring to the boil and return the oxtail to the pan. Add the bacon and the stock to cover – top up with water if necessary – and season with salt and pepper. Bring the liquid to a simmer and skim the surface well before covering with a cartouche of greaseproof paper.

Cook gently for 2½ hours until the meat is tender. Remove the pan from the heat and leave the oxtail to cool in the liquid.

Once the oxtail is cool enough to handle, take it out of the pan, along with the onion, celery and carrot, and set it aside. Pass the liquid through a sieve into a clean pan and put it back over the heat until reduced by half to make the sauce. Set the sauce aside.

Meanwhile, cut the cooked vegetables into small dice and pick the meat from the oxtail, discarding the bones. Mix the meat and vegetables well, then taste and season with salt and freshly ground pepper. If the mixture seems a little dry, add a couple of spoonfuls of the sauce.

Divide the oxtail mixture into 6 portions and lay the caul fat out on a board. Place the oxtail portions on the caul, spacing them out evenly, then tear the caul and gather it up around each portion to form a parcel. Place these on a tray and chill them in the fridge – leave them overnight if you can.

To serve, preheat the oven to 180°C/Fan 160°C/Gas 4. Place the oxtail parcels in an ovenproof dish and add enough of the sauce to cover the base of the dish – it should be about 1.5cm deep. Cook for about 30 minutes, basting the parcels with the sauce a few times. By the end of the cooking time the parcels should be hot in the centre and the pan practically dry. Serve hot with the rest of the sauce, reheated, and some mashed potato.

Oxtail Broth with Bone Marrow Dumplings

This is really two recipes in one. You can make and serve the delicious broth without the dumplings and you could also use the dumplings in a stew or soup. Together, they do make a truly wonderful dish.

Serves 4

2 tbsp	vegetable oil
8–10	pieces of oxtail
1	carrot, peeled and chopped
4	celery sticks, chopped
1	medium turnip, peeled and chopped
1	onion
2	bay leaves
1 tsp	cracked black pepper
2	cloves
4	garlic cloves
200ml	Madeira

Bone marrow dumplings

160g	bone marrow (soaked in iced water for 6 hours)
120g	plain flour, sifted
1 tsp	baking powder
1	shallot, finely chopped
120g	fresh white breadcrumbs
2	eggs, beaten
	salt and freshly ground black pepper

Heat the oil in a frying pan. Season the oxtail and fry it until well browned, then transfer it to a very large saucepan.

Add the carrot, celery and turnip to the frying pan and cook them until caramelised. Drain off any excess fat, then add the vegetables to the saucepan with the oxtail.

Cut the onion in half (do not peel) and place it cut-side down on a hot griddle with no oil until blackened. This will help to colour as well as flavour the broth. Add the onion to the pan along with the bay leaves, spices, garlic and Madeira. Generously cover the oxtail with cold water and bring to the boil.

Skim the surface and turn the heat down to a very gentle simmer – the liquid must not boil or the broth will be cloudy. Cook for 2½–3 hours, skimming regularly and topping up with hot water if necessary. The meat should be tender and falling off the bone, but check it with a skewer.

Take the pan off the heat and leave to cool slightly, then remove the oxtail and pass the broth through a fine sieve into a clean pan. Line the sieve with muslin if you want a really clear broth. Check the seasoning and add salt and pepper to taste.

To make the dumplings, remove the bone marrow from the iced water, chop it and place it in a bowl. Add the flour and baking powder, shallot, breadcrumbs and beaten eggs, then season with salt and pepper.

Knead the dough to bring it together, then place it on a floured surface and divide it into 12–16 balls. Bring the seasoned broth to the boil and carefully add the dumplings. Turn the heat down to a simmer, cover and cook the dumplings for 20 minutes.

Meanwhile, pick all the meat off the bones and reheat it in a separate pan with a little of the broth. To serve, put some meat into each bowl and ladle over the dumplings and broth.

Ox Heart Pastrami

Ox heart is cheap to buy and makes excellent pastrami. Although this recipe does take a while to complete there's actually very little effort involved – you just need to be patient while the brine and the spice crumb do their work. The pastrami is great in sandwiches, on toast or with salad and keeps well in the fridge for up to two weeks.

Serves 6–8

1	ox heart (about 2kg)
1 tbsp	black peppercorns
6	dried bay leaves
4	cloves
1 tbsp	thyme leaves
500g	sea salt
40g	sel rose (pink curing salt)
300g	light brown sugar
6	garlic cloves, peeled and crushed

Spice crumb

2 tbsp	cracked black pepper
1 tbsp	chopped juniper berries
1 tbsp	thyme leaves
2 tbsp	smoked paprika

Cut the heart in half down the middle and trim off any excess fat. Crush the peppercorns, bay leaves and cloves in a mortar and pestle or in a spice grinder and mix them with the thyme.

Pour 4 litres of water into a large saucepan and add the spice mixture, salts, sugar and garlic. Mix well and as soon as the water has come to the boil, remove the pan from the heat and leave the water to cool completely. Place the heart in a large plastic container and pour over the cold brine. Cover and refrigerate for 2 days, then turn the meat and leave it for another 2 days.

Take the heart out of the brine and rinse it well. Discard the brine. Place the heart in a large pan and cover it generously with cold water. Bring the water to the boil, skim, then turn the heat down to a very gentle simmer. Cook the heart for 2½ hours or until tender, then leave it to cool in the liquid.

Mix all the ingredients for the spice crumb together in a bowl.

Remove the cooled heart from the pan and pat it dry. Press the spice crumb into each piece, covering them completely. Wrap each half tightly in cling film and leave them in the fridge for 12 hours for best flavour. Slice thinly to serve.

Steak and Kidney Pudding

One of the great classics of British cooking, this is a real feast for a special occasion. The crust is perfect for mopping up the gravy and no other carbs are needed. Good with some green vegetables and a pint of Guinness or ale.

Serves 4

3 tbsp	plain flour
300g	ox kidney
600g	chuck steak
2 tbsp	vegetable oil
2	onions, peeled and diced
2	carrots, peeled and diced
2	celery sticks, diced
100g	button mushrooms
2 tbsp	brandy
1 tbsp	butter, plus extra for greasing
200ml	Guinness
600ml	veal stock
1 tbsp	Worcestershire sauce
1	bouquet garni
	salt and freshly ground black pepper

Suet pastry

225g	self-raising flour
115g	beef suet

Preheat the oven to 200°C/Fan 180°C/Gas 6. Spread the flour on a baking tray and put it in the preheated oven for 10 minutes until lightly browned. This will add flavour and colour to the gravy. Turn the oven down to 170°C/Fan 150°C/Gas 3½.

Trim the kidney and remove the core, then cut the kidney into 2cm pieces. Dice the chuck steak into pieces of a similar size and season everything well with salt and freshly ground pepper.

Heat a tablespoon of the oil in a casserole dish, add the diced onions, carrots and celery and brown them gently. Add the mushrooms and brown them as well.

Heat the remaining oil in a heavy frying pan and fry the kidney and the steak in small batches until well browned – don't overcrowd the pan. Drain each batch well and set aside. Deglaze the frying pan with the brandy, scraping up any sticky bits, and pour this into the casserole dish with the vegetables. Add the butter and the browned flour and mix well.

Slowly add the Guinness, mixing it in well to make a smooth sauce. Add the stock, Worcestershire sauce and the bouquet garni to the casserole dish, then the steak and kidney. Season with salt and pepper, then bring everything to a simmer and cover the dish with a lid. Place in the oven (170°C/Fan 150°C/Gas 3½) and cook for 2–3 hours until the meat is tender. Set aside to cool completely, preferably overnight.

To make the suet pastry, sift the flour into a bowl and add the suet, a pinch of salt and enough cold water to form a dough – you'll need 7–8 tablespoons. Cover and leave the pastry to rest for 30 minutes in the fridge.

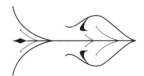

Roll the pastry into a circle big enough to line a 1-litre pudding basin. Cut out a quarter from the circle and reroll it into a round to form the lid. Butter the pudding basin and place the larger piece of pastry inside, pressing the edges together at the join to seal. Spoon in the steak and kidney mixture. Brush the top of the pastry with a little water and add the lid, pressing the edges together to seal. Trim off any excess.

Butter a square of greaseproof paper and lay it on top of the pudding. Take a piece of foil and make a small pleat in the middle to allow for expansion, cover the pudding and tie the foil in place. Place an upturned saucer or chef's ring in the bottom of a large saucepan and place the pudding on top. Add enough water to come three-quarters of the way up the basin and bring it to the boil. Cover the pan with a lid, reduce the heat to a simmer and steam the pudding for 3 hours. Check it regularly and top up with hot water as needed.

When the pudding is done, carefully remove the basin from the pan and take off the foil. Gently turn it out on to a serving dish.

Oriental Calf's Foot Salad

Texture is all here. With its spicy, zingy flavours and gelatinous meat, this is a take on the ubiquitous Hong Kong jellyfish salad.

Serves 4 as a starter

2	calves' feet		**Dressing**
4	star anise	80g	cashew nuts
2 tbsp	salt	1 tbsp	XO sauce
1 tbsp	cracked black pepper	1 tbsp	honey
2 tbsp	white vinegar		juice of 2 limes
2–3 tbsp	chopped fresh coriander	1 tbsp	sesame oil
2	red chillies, thinly sliced	2	spring onions, thinly sliced

Wash the feet well and burn off any hairs with a blowtorch. Place the feet in a large saucepan, cover with cold water and add the star anise, seasoning and the vinegar.

Bring the water to the boil, then turn down the heat and simmer the feet for 2 hours or until they're tender. Leave them to cool in the pan. Pick off all the meat, skin and gelatinous flesh and leave it in the fridge to chill.

Put the cashews in a dry frying pan and toast them until golden. Chop them roughly. Mix the XO sauce, honey, lime juice and oil to make the dressing and add the nuts and spring onions.

When the meat is cold and set, cut it into thin strips, put it in a bowl and mix it with the dressing. Sprinkle with chopped coriander and sliced chillies and serve.

Tetine de Veau with Tomato Relish

Tetine de veau is veal udder and although not easily found in Britain these days, it was common up until the early 1900s. Now udder is used only in processed meat products so we are still eating it but in disguise! In France and Italy it's sold pre-cooked (blanched) in speciality shops and can be served either hot or cold. I like to cook it in the following way.

Serves 4

200g	stale bread
2 tbsp	chopped parsley
1 tbsp	chopped thyme
400g	tetine de veau (veal udder)
100g	flour
1	egg, beaten
3 tbsp	vegetable oil
2 tbsp	butter
	salt and freshly ground black pepper

Tomato relish

6	ripe plum tomatoes
2 tbsp	olive oil
1	shallot, peeled and chopped
1	garlic clove, peeled and chopped
1 tsp	ground coriander
1 tbsp	tomato paste
1 tbsp	caster sugar
1 tbsp	Xérès (sherry) vinegar
1 tsp	Tabasco
2 tsp	Maldon sea salt

Blitz the bread to fine crumbs in a food processor with the herbs. Cut the udder into 1cm thick strips. Dust the strips in flour, dip them in the beaten egg and finally coat them in the crumbs.

Heat the oil and butter in a frying pan and fry the breaded strips until golden-brown and crispy. Drain them on kitchen paper and season with salt and pepper.

To make the tomato relish, place the tomatoes in boiling water for 20 seconds, then transfer them to a bowl of iced water to stop them cooking. Remove the skins then cut the tomatoes in half and scoop out the pips.

Heat the oil in a saucepan, add the chopped shallot, garlic and ground coriander and sweat until soft. Add the remaining ingredients, including the tomatoes, then cover the pan and simmer for 10 minutes.

Tip the tomato mixture into a blender and blitz until smooth. Serve the fried breaded strips with the tomato relish and a little salad of chopped coriander, mint and parsley

Beef Tendon Whisky Teriyaki

Beef tendon is popular in Asia but not often eaten in the UK. This is a shame as the meat is full of flavour, high in protein and low in fat. It's rich in collagen too so is very good for you. Tendons do need long slow cooking but once that's done you are in for a treat. Serve these as a starter with a glass of sake.

Serves 4

8	beef tendons
30g	fresh root ginger, sliced
2	garlic cloves, finely chopped
2 tbsp	clear honey
4 tbsp	whisky
3 tbsp	mirin
4 tbsp	dark soy sauce
1 tsp	chilli powder
	salt

Rinse the tendons in cold water, then place them in a large saucepan with the ginger. Generously cover them with water, add a little salt, then simmer for 3-4 hours until tender when pierced with a skewer but still with a little bite to them. You don't want to cook them to a mush. Leave the tendons to cool in the water, then drain, pat them dry and leave them in the fridge until needed.

If you have a pressure cooker you can cook the tendons in about an hour.

Mix the garlic, honey, whisky, mirin, soy sauce and chilli powder together in a bowl. Cut the cold tendons into pieces of about 6 x 2cm and add them to the bowl, then leave them to marinate for an hour.

Drain the tendons and put them on a baking tray under a hot grill. Cook them until sticky and glazed, basting them regularly with the marinade mixture.

If there is any marinade left once the tendons are done, pour it into a small pan, bring it to the boil and serve it with the tendons as a sauce.

Beef Tendon Meatballs

This is a good way of using beef tendon and these meatballs make an excellent snack with some tartare sauce. You can get all the preparation done well in advance, then fry the meatballs at the last minute.

Serves 4

6	beef tendons (about 500g)
200g	onglet, or hanger, steak
100g	white breadcrumbs
100g	plain flour
1	egg, beaten
	vegetable oil
	salt and freshly ground black pepper

Rinse the beef tendons in cold water, then place them in a large saucepan, add water to cover them and season with a little salt. Gently simmer the tendons for about 3 hours or until tender when pierced with a skewer. Leave the tendons to cool in the water.

If you have a pressure cooker you can cook the tendons in about an hour.

Once the tendons are cool, pat them dry, put them on a plate and leave them in the fridge for a couple of hours until set. Then mince the steak and tendons together through the medium setting on your mincer. Season, add a tablespoon of breadcrumbs, then mix everything together well.

Using your hands shape the mixture into walnut-sized balls. Roll the balls in flour, dip them in the beaten egg and then into the remaining breadcrumbs.

Half-fill a large saucepan or a deep-fat fryer with oil and heat to 180°C. Deep-fry the meatballs until golden and cooked through – this should take 3–4 minutes. Cook them in a few batches so you don't overcrowd the pan, draining each batch on kitchen paper.

Serve the meatballs with some tartare sauce (see page 254).

Tripe with Apple and Onions

A French classic, this is perfect winter food – good with boiled potatoes. It's a little laborious but well worth the effort. Honeycomb tripe comes from the reticulum, the cow's second stomach, and has a beautiful honeycomb structure that gives it its name.

Serves 6

1kg	honeycomb tripe
1	calf's foot, split in half (ask your butcher to do this)
300g	pork skin (no fat)
2 sprigs	thyme
3	cloves
2	bay leaves
2 litres	dry cider
1 tbsp	butter
4	onions, peeled and sliced
1	large leek (white part only), sliced
1	large carrot, peeled and sliced
2	celery sticks, sliced
1	Bramley apple, peeled and sliced
1	eating apple (Cox or Golden), peeled and sliced
4	garlic cloves, peeled and chopped
2 tbsp	Dijon mustard
50ml	Calvados
1 bunch	flatleaf parsley, chopped
	salt and freshly ground black pepper

Rinse the tripe well in cold water. Place it in a very large saucepan with the calf's foot, pork skin, thyme, cloves and bay leaves and add a little salt. Pour over the cider, then add water to cover the tripe by at least 6cm.

Bring to the boil, skim and turn the heat down to a gentle simmer. Loosely cover the saucepan, allowing some steam to escape, and cook the tripe for 2 hours. Take the pan off the heat.

When the tripe is cool enough to handle, remove it and strain, keeping the cooking liquid. Discard the thyme, cloves and bay leaves and allow the cooking liquid to cool, then skim any fat off the surface.

Cut the tripe and skin into 5–6cm squares. Pick the skin and meat off the foot and cut them to the same size. The skin, tripe and foot will still be quite firm but this is fine.

Heat the butter in a large saucepan, add the vegetables, apples and garlic and sweat them until tender and lightly caramelised. Add all the meat and the cooking liquid, partially cover the pan and simmer for another 2½ hours. Alternatively, put everything into a casserole dish, bring the liquid to a simmer and cook in the oven at 180°C/Fan 160°C/Gas 4 for 2 hours.

Take the pan off the heat or remove the dish from the oven and allow to cool slightly, then stir in the Dijon mustard and Calvados. Sprinkle over with lots of freshly chopped parsley and serve with boiled potatoes.

Tripe with Buckwheat

*This recipe, using chitterlings (intestines) as well as tripe,
is Russian in origin and makes a hearty bowl of goodness.
Pig's chitterlings are best, but you can also use beef or lamb
chitterlings or a mixture.*

Serves 4

500g	tripe and chitterlings
200g	buckwheat
3 tbsp	butter
2	onions, peeled and chopped
1 tbsp	chopped fresh marjoram
	salt and freshly ground black pepper

Rinse the tripe and chitterlings well and put them in a large saucepan. Cover with plenty of cold water, add salt and bring to the boil. Cook the tripe and chitterlings until tender, then drain, reserving the cooking liquid. Chop the meat into very small pieces or put it through a mincer.

Boil the buckwheat in plenty of water for 20–30 minutes until cooked, then drain it and set it aside.

Melt the butter in a saucepan, add the onions and sweat them until cooked. Add the tripe and chitterlings and continue to cook until they start to caramelise and take on some colour. Add the buckwheat and season well – be very generous with the pepper.

Moisten the mixture with a little of the cooking liquid, then simmer for 10 minutes. Add marjoram to taste, then serve.

Braised Tripe with Red Pepper and Basil

You can prepare this excellent tripe dish the day before you need it and just reheat it when you're ready to eat. Boiled potatoes are the perfect accompaniment or you could pile everything into a dish and top it with puff pastry to make a tasty pie. Some butchers sell tripe precooked.

Serves 4

800g	honeycomb tripe
1	onion, peeled and halved
1	carrot, peeled and halved
3	celery sticks
3	red peppers
1 tbsp	olive oil
2	red onions, peeled and sliced
1 tbsp	tomato paste
6	plum tomatoes, peeled and deseeded
50ml	white wine
750ml	chicken stock
2 tbsp	torn basil leaves
2 tbsp	roughly chopped flatleaf parsley
	salt and freshly ground black pepper

Rinse the tripe and put it in a large pan of salted water with the onion, carrot and 1 of the celery sticks. Bring the water to the boil, then reduce the heat and simmer the tripe for 3 hours or until tender. Leave it to cool in the water.

Slice the remaining celery sticks. Peel the peppers with a vegetable peeler and slice them. Heat the oil in a wide pan and add the celery, peppers and red onions. Cook them over a gentle heat for 8–10 minutes without letting them colour.

Stir in the tomato paste and tomatoes, then turn up the heat. Add the white wine and reduce it quickly before adding the stock. Bring the stock to a simmer. Cut the tripe into pieces measuring about 4cm and add them to the pan. Simmer for at least 30 minutes.

Season well with salt and pepper and add the herbs just before serving with some boiled potatoes.

Crispy Fried Tripe with Piquillo Mayonnaise

Don't tell your guests what this is and just watch them enjoy the crispy delicious morsels! I've suggested cayenne here but you can experiment with different spices as you like. And if you can find precooked tripe, this is a really easy recipe.

Serves 4

400g	honeycomb tripe
1	onion, peeled and cut in half
1	carrot, peeled and cut in half
1	celery stick
150g	potato flour
1 tbsp	cayenne pepper
	vegetable oil, for frying
	salt

Piquillo mayonnaise

60g	piquillo peppers (from a jar), drained
200g	mayonnaise
½ tsp	cayenne pepper

Rinse the tripe and put it in a large pan of salted water with the onion, carrot and celery. Bring the water to the boil, then reduce the heat and simmer the tripe for 3 hours or until tender. Leave it to cool in the water.

Meanwhile, make the piquillo mayonnaise. Blitz the peppers in a food processor to make a purée. Mix this into the mayonnaise and season with the cayenne and some salt.

Once the tripe is cool, cut it into strips about 1cm wide. Mix the potato flour, cayenne and 2 teaspoons of salt together in a bowl and dust the tripe strips with this mixture. Half-fill a large saucepan or a deep-fat fryer with oil and heat it to 180°C. Fry the tripe in small batches in the hot oil for a couple of minutes until golden and crispy.

Serve at once with the spicy piquillo mayonnaise.

Leberknodel

These Bavarian liver dumplings can be made with any kind of liver, but calf's liver works best in my view. They are traditionally served with sauerkraut or in a bowl of beautiful beef broth.

Serves 4

2 tbsp	butter
1	onion, peeled and finely chopped
1 tsp	dried marjoram
80g	stale bread
	milk
250g	calf's liver, trimmed
1	egg, beaten
	grated zest of ½ lemon
1 tbsp	chopped parsley
2 tbsp	plain flour
	salt and freshly ground black pepper

To serve

1 litre	beef broth (see page 260)

Melt the butter in a frying pan and sweat the onion until soft, but don't let it brown. Add the marjoram, remove the pan from the heat and leave the onion to cool.

Put the bread in a bowl and add enough milk to moisten it. When it's soft, squeeze out any excess milk and add the bread to the onions.

Mince or finely chop the liver and add it to the onions and bread. Mix in the egg, lemon zest and parsley, then season with salt and plenty of pepper. Add as much of the flour as you need to if the mixture seems loose, then shape it into balls about the size of a golfball.

Bring a pan of salted water to simmering point. Drop the balls into the water and when they rise, flip them over and cook for a total of 7–8 minutes. Carefully remove them with a slotted spoon and serve them in a bowl of steaming hot beef broth (see page 260).

Alternatively, you can fry the balls in a little oil until brown and crispy, then add them to the broth.

Braised Stuffed Oxtail

This is a splendid dish for a special feast. There's quite a bit of work, but most of it can be done the day before you want to serve the oxtail, so it's ideal for a party.

Serves 8

2	oxtails (about 1.5kg each), including bones
	splash of brandy
	caul fat to make a sheet 30 x 30cm
	butter
	vegetable oil
2	celery sticks, diced
2	onions, peeled and chopped
1	carrot, peeled and diced
2	garlic cloves, peeled
1 bottle	full-bodied red wine
250ml	port
1	bouquet garni
100g	smoked bacon, diced
1 litre	veal stock
	salt and freshly ground black pepper

Stuffing

60g	smoked bacon
200g	pork fillet
100g	pork belly (fatty)
100g	pork fat
1 sprig	thyme
	grating of nutmeg

Trim some of the excess fat from the thick end of the oxtails. Chop off the thinnest part so you are left with a length of about 25cm. Turn the oxtail upside down so the smooth side is on the work surface. Using a sharp boning knife, carefully follow the bone structure from one end to the other removing the bone as you do so. This is a tricky job, so go slowly and take care not to make too many holes. The result should look like an oblong carpet, not a string vest! Repeat with the other oxtail. If you have a helpful butchers' shop nearby, you might be able to get them to bone the oxtails for you.

Keep the bones and the thin part of the tails for braising. Put the tail meat in a bowl, season it with salt and pepper and douse with brandy. Then cover the bowl with cling film and refrigerate the meat for an hour.

Meanwhile, make the stuffing. Remove the rind from the smoked bacon and dice it with the fillet, belly and fat. Put it all through a mincer with a medium-sized (4mm) plate. Pick the leaves off the thyme and mix them into the stuffing, then season with salt, pepper and a grating of nutmeg and beat well. Take a spoonful of mixture and fry it quickly until cooked, then taste to check the seasoning.

Rinse the caul fat and lay it flat on a clean work surface. Put an oxtail, skin-side down, on the centre of the caul. Shape the stuffing into a sausage and place it on the oxtail. Put the other oxtail on top then roll the caul fat tightly around everything. Using butchers' string, tie the caul in place lengthways and across at regular intervals to make a neat, tight sausage.

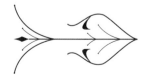

Heat a tablespoon each of butter and oil in a pan that's wide enough to hold the oxtail. Add the oxtail and lightly brown it all over. Remove the oxtail from the pan and add the bones, vegetables and garlic with a little more oil if needed. When these are caramelised, add the wine, port, bouquet garni and smoked bacon, then season. Bring to the boil. Add the oxtail and veal stock, then bring the liquid back to the boil. Skim, partially cover the pan, then leave the oxtail to simmer for 2½ hours until the meat is tender. Leave it to cool in the liquid.

When the oxtail is cool enough to handle, take it out and set the liquid aside. Gently remove the strings from the oxtail and roll it tightly in cling film to make a perfect sausage shape. Chill it in the fridge overnight.

Pass the cooking liquid through a fine sieve and then pour it into a saucepan and reduce over a high heat until it has the consistency of a sauce. Skim all the fat that comes to the surface. Finish the sauce with a little butter to give it a shine and a lovely velvety finish.

Cut the oxtail into 3cm slices, put them on a plate and cover with cling film. Reheat in a steamer, then serve with the sauce and mashed potato.

L'AGNEAU

L'AGNEAU: *sheep and lamb*

In some countries they eat much more sheep offal than we do in the UK. The type most commonly seen here is lamb's liver, which can be excellent, but sadly is often overcooked. I remember horrible leathery liver from my school days but it doesn't have to be like that! Liver that comes from a young animal, and has been cooked briefly so it is still pink inside, is sweet and delicious. Try cooking devilled lamb's liver – and kidneys – and you'll find you have a treat.

Sheep and lamb offal, like that of all animals, is generally cheap and highly nutritious. Lamb's hearts have become popular again and are now stocked by supermarkets. They are excellent stuffed – see page 224. Sheep's trotters have a milder flavour than pig's trotters but have an equally wonderful gelatinous texture, and lamb's brains can be prepared in the same way as calf's brains.

One of the great lamb offal dishes is, of course, haggis, which uses the heart, liver and lungs, all encased in the animal's stomach. These parts are highly perishable and need to be used quickly – hence the tradition of haggis, which was made after an animal was slaughtered and ensured that nothing went to waste.

All the recipes in this chapter can also be cooked with goat offal, which can be excellent. Goat lungs, though, are an acquired taste. They're my mother-in-law's favourite, and whenever I cook a goat in France I save the lungs for her. She eats them pan-fried with garlic and parsley or stewed in a cream sauce. I don't expect you to go that far but do try some of the recipes in this chapter and discover the joys of lamb and sheep offal.

Curried Lambs' Kidneys

This makes a quick, economical and very flavoursome supper dish. If you like your food really hot and spicy, you could add some extra curry powder.

Serves 4

8	lambs' kidneys, outer layer of fat removed
1 tbsp	vegetable oil
20g	butter
1 tsp	curry powder
½ tsp	garam masala
1	red onion, peeled and finely chopped
2	garlic cloves, peeled and finely chopped
75ml	white wine
250ml	double cream
3 tbsp	chopped coriander
	salt and freshly ground black pepper

Slice the kidneys in half and cut out the white cores. Cut each half into 2 pieces and season with salt and pepper. Heat the oil in a frying pan, add the kidney pieces and fry them very quickly over a high heat until browned all over. Drain the kidneys in a colander – this is important, as the juices can be quite strong – and set them aside.

Return the pan to a medium heat and add the butter. Add the curry powder and garam masala and toast them lightly, then add the chopped onion and cook for 3 minutes. Add the garlic and cook gently for another 2 minutes.

Add the white wine and continue to cook until the wine has reduced by two-thirds. Add the cream and reduce to a light sauce consistency. Check the seasoning and add salt and pepper to taste.

Return the drained kidneys to the sauce and reheat them gently. Once they are hot, add the chopped coriander and serve with plain rice.

Devilled Lamb's Liver on Toast

*Lamb's liver is readily available and very reasonably priced.
This quick and easy way of preparing it makes a lovely starter
or lunch dish. You need good thick slices of sourdough.*

Serves 4

4 slices	sourdough bread
	flour, for dusting
500g	lamb's liver, trimmed and cut into strips
2 tbsp	olive oil
25g	butter
5	shallots, peeled and finely chopped
¾ tbsp	English mustard
2 pinches	cayenne pepper
1 tbsp	Worcestershire sauce
150ml	double cream
	salt and freshly ground black pepper

Grill the sourdough bread on a griddle pan and keep it warm. Spread the flour on a plate and season it with salt and pepper. Dust the strips of liver with flour.

Heat the olive oil in a large frying pan. Add the liver and cook it for 2–3 minutes on each side – it should remain pink. Remove the liver from the pan and cover it lightly to keep it warm.

Melt the butter in the frying pan and add the shallots. Sauté them briefly, then stir in the mustard, cayenne and Worcestershire sauce. Add the double cream and cook until it has reduced slightly and the sauce has a coating consistency. Check the seasoning and add more if necessary. Return the cooked, drained liver to the pan and reheat, coating it all in the sauce.

Serve the liver on the warm grilled sourdough toast.

Devilled Kidneys

Once a traditional country house breakfast dish, devilled kidneys are hearty, warming winter food. They make a great supper with some boiled potatoes and winter greens.

Serves 4

16	lambs' kidneys, outer layer of fat removed
2–3 tbsp	olive oil
3	shallots, peeled and finely chopped
1 tbsp	Dijon mustard
1 tbsp	Worcestershire sauce
	Tabasco sauce
150ml	double cream
	salt and freshly ground black pepper

Slice the kidneys in half. Cut out the white cores and discard them.

Heat a tablespoon of the oil in a frying pan. Season the kidneys all over and fry them for about 3 minutes on each side until nicely coloured – add more oil if you need it. Drain the kidneys in a colander – this is important, as the juices can be quite strong. Cover the kidneys lightly and set them aside to keep warm.

Return the pan to the heat and add another tablespoon of oil. Add the shallots and cook for 2–3 minutes over a gentle heat, then add the mustard, Worcestershire sauce, a dash of Tabasco and the cream to the pan and bring to the boil.

Check the seasoning and add more Tabasco if you like. Return the kidneys to the pan for a moment or two to heat through, then serve.

Moroccan-style Lamb Kebabs

These make a nice change for a barbecue and if you pile the meat into wraps or pitta no one will realise it's offal! The kidney fat is there to moisten the liver and hearts, but if you prefer you can use streaky bacon instead.

Serves 4

500g	lamb's liver, trimmed
500g	lambs' hearts, trimmed and diced
150g	lamb's kidney fat, diced
3	garlic cloves, finely chopped
1 tbsp	chopped flatleaf parsley
2 tsp	ground cumin
1½ tsp	paprika
	salt and freshly ground black pepper

Cut the liver, hearts and fat into 3cm cubes and put them in a bowl. Add the remaining ingredients, mix well and leave to marinate for at least 2 hours, stirring regularly.

Meanwhile, soak some wooden skewers in cold water.

Thread the meats on to the skewers alternating pieces of liver, heart and fat. Ideally, cook the kebabs on a barbecue for 3 or 4 minutes on each side, but you can also cook them under a preheated grill. Take care not to overcook them – they are best left slightly pink.

Serve the kebabs with a large salad or remove the meat from the skewers and serve it in wraps or pitta bread.

Haggis

This traditional Scottish dish came into being as a way of using the perishable innards of an animal as soon as possible. It's made with the heart, liver and lungs - known as the pluck - of a lamb and cooked in the stomach of the animal. Seasoning is very important - particularly pepper. I also like to use a four-spice blend - also known as quatre épices - which is a classic sausage seasoning made up of cinnamon, cloves, pepper and nutmeg. Tatties and neeps - boiled potatoes and turnips - are the classic accompaniment for this splendid feast.

Serves 10

	heart, liver and lungs (pluck) of a new season's lamb
20g	butter
3	onions, peeled and chopped
200g	suet
250g	coarse oatmeal
2 tsp	ground allspice
1 tsp	4 spice mix
1 tbsp	ground black pepper
500ml	chicken stock
1	lamb's stomach, well rinsed
	salt

Rinse the pluck well in several changes of cold water. Place it in a pan, add cold water to cover and season with salt. Bring the water to the boil and skim the surface, then reduce the heat and gently simmer the pluck for 2 hours. Remove the pan from the heat and leave the pluck to cool in the liquid.

Melt the butter in a frying pan, add the chopped onions and cook them until translucent. Tip them into a large bowl and leave them to cool.

Remove the cooled pluck from the pan. Take out and discard the windpipe, then cut the heart, lungs and liver into pieces. Mince the meat coarsely.

Mix the suet, oatmeal and spices together, then add the minced meat and stock. Stir well.

Turn the washed stomach inside out so the coarse side is inside and tie one end. Fill the stomach with the mixture and tie or stitch up loosely, leaving plenty of room for expansion.

Make a pleat in a big sheet of foil and wrap the haggis up in it. The foil protects the haggis as it cooks – otherwise the sides might touch the pan causing the haggis to burst.

Put a plate or a folded tea towel in the bottom of a large saucepan. Half-fill the pan with water, add salt and bring the water to a gentle simmer. Carefully add the haggis and leave it poach in the simmering water, uncovered, for 3 hours.

At the end of the cooking time, gently remove the haggis and unwrap the foil. Bring the haggis to the table on a large plate for your guests to admire, then split it open to serve – spectacular!

Lamb Brain Beignets with Pepper Coulis

If you haven't cooked brains before, this is a great recipe to start with. Lamb brains have a nice delicate flavour and crisp up beautifully when deep-fried. Serve them as a starter with the pepper coulis.

Serves 4

4	lamb brains
1	lemon
1	bay leaf
1 sprig	thyme
80g	cornflour
80g	plain flour
120ml	cold sparkling water
	vegetable oil, for frying
	salt

Pepper coulis

8	garlic cloves, peeled
1	shallot, peeled
	olive oil
200g	piquillo peppers (from a jar or can)
	sherry vinegar
	Tabasco sauce
	salt

Soak the brains in ice-cold water for an hour, then place them in a saucepan with a couple of slices of lemon, the bay leaf, thyme, and a generous pinch of salt. Add cold water to cover, then bring to the boil and simmer for 5 minutes. Leave the brains to cool in the pan.

When the brains are cool enough to handle, take them out of the liquid and separate each brain in half, carefully peeling away any dark membrane. Place them on kitchen paper to dry.

Whisk the cornflour and plain flour with the sparkling water but do not over work it.

Half-fill a large saucepan or a deep-fat fryer with oil and heat to 180°C. Dip the brains in the batter, add them to the oil and deep-fry for about 3 minutes or until golden and really crisp. It's best to do this in batches so you don't overcrowd the pan. Drain the brains on kitchen paper and season with a little salt. Serve with the pepper coulis.

To make the pepper coulis, preheat the oven to 200°C/Fan 180°C/Gas 6. Place the peeled garlic and shallot on a piece of foil. Season with a little salt and add a drizzle of olive oil. Fold over the foil to enclose the garlic and shallot completely, then bake in the oven for 35 minutes by which time they should be soft and golden. Remove and leave to cool.

Put the garlic and shallot with any oil and juices in a blender and add the drained piquillo peppers. Blitz to a fine purée, adding olive oil, vinegar and Tabasco to taste.

Tartare of Lambs' Hearts with Mint Pesto

The classic tartare is made with beef, but you can use any meat as long as it is really fresh and properly prepared. This is a lovely flavour combination – sweet and smoky, perfectly set off by the freshness of the mint.

Serves 4

8	lambs' hearts, as fresh as possible
2 tbsp	smoked rapeseed oil
	flaked sea salt
	chilli flakes
	micro herbs, such as mint and lemon verbena

Mint pesto

1 bunch	mint
½ bunch	flatleaf parsley
3	anchovy fillets
	juice and grated zest of 1 lemon
6	ice cubes
60ml	olive oil

To make the mint pesto, put the washed mint and parsley in a blender with the anchovies, lemon juice and zest and the ice cubes. Blitz everything together, then drizzle in the olive oil. When you have a smooth pesto, scoop it out of the blender into a bowl and put it in the fridge to chill.

Trim the hearts to remove any sinew or fat, then chop them into neat, tiny pieces, about 3mm. Gently fold in the smoked oil.

To serve, spread some mint pesto on cold plates, sprinkle chopped heart on top and season with a little flaked sea salt and some chilli flakes. Finish with the micro herbs. Some grilled sourdough bread is nice with this.

Stuffed Lambs' Hearts with Mint Dressing

Most good butchers sell lambs' hearts and they are available in some supermarkets now too. Best cooked long and slow, they make perfect little vehicles for stuffing. It is important to use new-season young lamb – older lamb or mutton hearts have too strong a taste.

Serves 4

4	new-season lamb's hearts
1 tbsp	olive oil
1	onion, peeled and diced
1	carrot, peeled and diced
1	celery stick, diced
125ml	white wine
700ml	brown chicken stock
1 small	bouquet garni
60g	butter
	salt and freshly ground black pepper

Stuffing

50g	fresh breadcrumbs (preferably sourdough)
2 tbsp	flatleaf parsley, chopped
2 tbsp	fresh mint, chopped
3	shallots, peeled and finely chopped
2	garlic cloves, peeled and finely chopped
3 tbsp	olive oil

Dressing

	juice and zest of 1 lemon
2 tbsp	mint, chopped
2 tbsp	parsley, chopped
120ml	olive oil

Preheat the oven to 200°C/Fan 180°C/Gas 6. Trim any fat away from the top of the hearts, then rinse and dry them well.

Mix together the ingredients for the stuffing and season well with salt and pepper. Stuff each heart tightly with the mixture, making sure it goes right to the bottom of the cavity. Stitch the top of each heart with some butcher's string to prevent any of the stuffing from falling out.

Heat a wide ovenproof pan or casserole dish and add the olive oil. Season the hearts, add them to the pan and carefully brown them on each side. Remove the hearts from the pan and set them aside. Add the onion, carrot and celery to the pan and colour them lightly, then add the wine and cook until the wine is reduced by three-quarters.

Pour in the stock and put the stuffed hearts back in the pan together with the bouquet garni. Bring to a simmer, cover the pan and place it in the preheated oven for 2 hours. Turn the hearts after the first hour. Once the hearts are cooked, leave them to cool in the liquid.

Mix together the dressing ingredients and season with salt and pepper. Keep the dressing at room temperature.

Remove the hearts from the pan and carefully remove the string. Pass the cooking liquid through a fine sieve into a saucepan and cook until reduced by half. Add the butter to the sauce to thicken it, then remove the pan from the heat and set it aside, covered.

Put the hearts in a pan with 3 or 4 tablespoons of the sauce and place it over the heat. Keep rolling and turning the hearts in the sauce until they are warmed through and beautifully shiny and sticky on the outside. Serve with the remaining sauce on the side and the mint dressing.

Lambs' Testicles with Lemon and Capers

Testicles are eaten in many countries but they are often called something innocuous so as not to put off diners! Lambs' testicles are usually referred to as 'fries' or 'stones'. A by-product of the castration of young animals raised for meat, testicles would once have been a seasonal dish, available in late spring, but frozen ones are now available all year round.

Serves 4

4	lambs' testicles
1 sprig	thyme
2	bay leaves
2	lemons
	plain flour, for dusting
½ tbsp	vegetable oil
2 tbsp	butter
2–3 tbsp	chopped parsley
1	shallot, peeled and chopped
1 tbsp	capers
	salt and freshly ground black pepper

Place the testicles in a pan of cold water with the thyme and bay leaves and season with salt. Bring the water to the boil, then turn the heat down to a very gentle simmer for 10 minutes. Take the pan off the heat and leave the testicles to cool slightly.

Meanwhile, segment the lemons. Cut the ends off a lemon and stand it upright on one end. Using a sharp knife, slice down the lemon to remove the peel and much of the white pith as you can. Holding the peeled lemon over a bowl to catch any juice, slice between the membranes to release each segment. When you're done, squeeze any juice from the membranes into the bowl. Repeat with the other lemon.

When the testicles are cool enough to handle, peel off the skin. Cut the testicles into 2 or 3 thick slices and dust them in flour. Heat the oil and butter in a frying pan and fry the testicles until golden and crisp on both sides. Remove them from the pan and set them aside to keep warm.

Add the lemon segments and juice to the pan with the chopped parsley, shallot and capers. Season with salt and pepper, then simmer for 2–3 minutes. Pour the sauce over the testicles and serve at once.

Salad of Lambs' Tongues and Cucumber

Lambs' tongues are cheap to buy and are very tender and delicious to eat. This dish looks beautiful and makes the most of the delicate flavour of both tongues and cucumber.

Serves 4 as a starter

8	lambs' tongues
1	onion, peeled and cut in half
1	celery stick
1	bouquet garni (thyme, bay and parsley stalks)
	a few whole peppercorns
3	cucumbers
2	egg yolks
1 tbsp	Dijon mustard
20ml	white wine vinegar
300ml	light olive oil
200ml	rapeseed oil
1 punnet	lamb's lettuce, washed
	salt and freshly ground black pepper

Wash the tongues well and place them in a pan of cold water. Bring the water to the boil, then reduce the heat to a simmer and skim the surface. Add the onion, celery and bouquet garni, then season with a good pinch of salt and a few whole peppercorns. Cook the tongues gently for about an hour until tender – check with the tip of a knife. Leave them to cool slightly and then, while they are still warm, peel off the rough outer skin. Set the tongues aside to cool completely.

Peel the cucumbers, keeping the skin in long strips. Bring a pan of salted water to the boil and blanch the cucumber skin for 2 minutes. Drain and refresh the skin in iced water to stop the cooking process and keep the colour. Drain well.

Put the cucumber skins in a blender with the egg yolks, mustard, white wine vinegar and a pinch of salt. Add a splash of water and blend well. With the blender running, very slowly add the olive oil and rapeseed oil in a gentle stream. If the dressing starts to get very thick, add a little more water. You want a pale-green mayonnaise-style dressing

Cut 2 of the cucumbers in half and scoop out the seeds. Cut the cucumbers into half-moon slices. Using a peeler, cut ribbons of the remaining cucumber, discarding the seeds. Slice the tongues thinly.

Mix the cucumber slices with some of the dressing and lay them on a large platter. Place the tongue slices over them and top with some of the cucumber ribbons, curling them around the tongue. Mix the rest of the dressing with the salad leaves and the remaining cucumber ribbons and add this to the platter. Season with salt and pepper and serve at once.

Pickled Lambs' Tongues with Potato Salad

Pickling used to be a really popular way of preparing lambs' tongues. They're great as picnic food or for a summer salad.

Serves 4

8	lambs' tongues
	juice of 1 lemon
500ml	cider vinegar
260g	caster sugar
2	cloves
12	peppercorns
1	bay leaf
6	juniper berries
	salt

Potato salad

12	new potatoes (Jersey Royals), washed
12	small heritage tomatoes, quartered
2	shallots, peeled and sliced
3 tbsp	chopped flatleaf parsley
4 tbsp	mayonnaise
2 tbsp	red wine vinegar
	salt and freshly ground black pepper

Rinse the tongues under cold running water for 5 minutes. Place them in a pan, cover with cold water and add the lemon juice and a tablespoon of salt. Bring the water to the boil, then turn down the heat and simmer for about 2 hours or until the tongues are tender. Leave the tongues to cool.

Drain the tongues, then peel off the skin. Place the tongues in a large sterilised Kilner jar.

Put the vinegar, sugar, spices, bay leaf, juniper berries and a tablespoon of salt in a saucepan, add 200ml of water and bring everything to the boil. Pour this mixture over the tongues, then seal the jar and refrigerate for at least 5 days before using.

To make the potato salad, bring a saucepan of water to the boil and add the potatoes and salt. Cover the pan and simmer the potatoes for 20 minutes or until tender, then drain.

Cut the potatoes into thick slices and put them in a bowl. Add the tomatoes, shallots and parsley, then fold in the mayonnaise and vinegar. Season with salt and pepper.

Slice the tongues and serve with the potato salad.

Ragout of Lambs' Sweetbreads, Kidneys and Saffron

Lambs' sweetbreads are the pancreas and thymus glands of the animal and are prized for their delicate flavour and creamy texture. This is a tasty, rustic dish and is best served in bowls with some couscous or flatbread.

Serves 4

1kg	lambs' sweetbreads
1 tbsp	white wine vinegar or squeeze of lemon juice
2 tbsp	olive oil
200g	button onions, peeled
½ tsp	cumin seeds
50ml	white wine
20ml	Madeira
50ml	orange juice
4	plum tomatoes, peeled, deseeded and chopped
2 pinches	saffron
700ml	chicken stock
120g	butter
	flour, for dusting
6	lambs' kidneys
	salt and freshly ground black pepper

Put the sweetbreads in a saucepan of cold water with a tablespoon of white wine vinegar or a squeeze of lemon juice. Bring the water to the boil, then simmer for a couple of minutes. Drain the sweetbreads and leave to cool, then peel off the membrane.

Heat a tablespoon of the oil in a wide saucepan. Add the button onions and cook them until golden brown all over, then add the cumin seeds and toast them with the onions. Add the wine and Madeira to deglaze the pan, then boil until the liquid is reduced by half. Add the orange juice and chopped tomatoes together with the saffron and season well. Add the stock, bring to a simmer and continue to cook gently until the onions are tender. Remove the onions from the pan and set them aside. Reduce the liquid by half, then stir in half the butter to thicken the sauce. Return the onions to the sauce.

Slice the kidneys in half and cut out the white cores. Cut each half into 2 pieces and season well. Heat a heavy pan with the remaining tablespoon of olive oil and fry the kidneys for a couple of minutes, colouring them well on all sides. Remove the kidneys from the pan and set them aside.

In the same pan gently heat the rest of the butter until it starts to foam. Dust the sweetbreads in seasoned flour and carefully add them to the pan. Cook them for 4–5 minutes until golden-brown all over, then remove them from the pan and drain on kitchen paper.

Add the kidneys to the pan of onions and sauce and reheat them gently. Place the sweetbreads in a warm dish and pour over the kidneys and sauce.

Sheep's Trotter Salad 'Alain Chapel'

When I was learning my trade, I worked as a commis chef for the great Alain Chapel at his Mionnay restaurant. This delicious sheep's trotter dish was a favourite and was regularly cooked for friends and family. The sauce is also good served with cold meat, asparagus or as a dip for crudités.

Serves 6 as a starter or a light main course

20	sheep's trotters
1 sprig	thyme
200ml	white wine vinegar
3 tbsp	olive oil
1 tbsp	red wine vinegar
3	hard-boiled eggs
	salt and freshly ground black pepper

Sauce

100ml	red wine vinegar, plus an extra splash
20g	plain flour
3	egg yolks
1 tbsp	Dijon mustard
220ml	vegetable oil
2 tbsp	Worcestershire sauce
250ml	crème fraiche

Wash the trotters well and burn off any hairs with a blowtorch. Place the trotters in a large saucepan with cold water to cover, then add a tablespoon of salt and the thyme and white wine vinegar.

Bring the water to the boil, then turn down the heat and simmer for 2 hours or until the trotters are tender. Leave the trotters to cool, then drain them and remove all the bones. Cut the trotters into strips and put them in a bowl, then dress with the olive oil and the tablespoon of red wine vinegar. Season with salt and pepper and set aside.

To make the sauce, pour the 100ml of vinegar into a small saucepan and whisk in the flour. Quickly bring the mixture to the boil, whisking continuously to avoid lumps. Take the pan off the heat, cover and leave to cool to room temperature.

Whisk the egg yolks with the mustard and a splash of red wine vinegar in a bowl and season with salt and pepper. Slowly add the oil to make a mayonnaise. Now whisk this into the flour and vinegar mixture along with the Worcestershire sauce and crème fraiche. The texture should be like double cream – add a little water if it is too stiff. Check the seasoning and add salt and pepper to taste.

Arrange the trotters on a platter and pour the sauce around them. Scatter over the chopped hard-boiled eggs and serve.

Sheep's Trotter Poulette

Poulette sauce is a classic cream sauce with mushrooms. It's just right with these trotters and can also be served with chicken and with boiled meats.

Serves 4

12	sheep's trotters
2	carrots, peeled
2	turnips, peeled
2 sprigs	parsley, stalks and leaves separated
2 sprigs	thyme
2	bay leaves
1 tbsp	white peppercorns
4	cloves
2 tbsp	butter
2	onions, peeled and sliced
2 tbsp	plain flour
24	button mushrooms, cleaned
3	egg yolks
200ml	double cream
	juice of 1 lemon
	salt and white pepper

Wash the trotters well and burn off any hairs with a blowtorch. Place the trotters in a saucepan, add the carrots, turnips, parsley stalks, thyme and bay leaves, then generously cover with cold water. Season with salt, white peppercorns and cloves, bring to the boil then skim any scum from the surface. Turn the heat down to a very gentle simmer and cook the trotters for 2–3 hours or until tender. Leave the trotters to cool slightly, then remove them from the pan. Strain the liquid and set it aside.

Pull out the largest bone from each of the trotters. Leave the smaller bones in place so the trotters keep their shape. Keep the trotters warm while you prepare the sauce poulette.

Melt the butter in a saucepan, add the sliced onions and fry them until coloured. Add the flour and mix well, then add 1 litre of the reserved cooking liquid. Bring to the boil, skim, then gently simmer for 20 minutes. Add the button mushrooms and continue to simmer for another 10 minutes.

Mix the yolks and cream together, then pour them into the pan. Stir and continue to cook the sauce for 5 minutes, but do not allow it to boil.

Season the sauce with salt, pepper and lemon juice, then add the chopped parsley leaves. Pour the sauce over the warm trotters and serve the dish with garlic croutons (see page 253).

Lamb's Head, Oyster and Bacon Pie

Maybe not a dish to make every day but this pie is wholesome, delicious and, even with the oysters, an economical way of feeding eight people. Serve hot with buttered cabbage or kale or cold with a pint of bitter!

Serves 8

2	lambs' heads, split in half
6	bay leaves
1	carrot, peeled and quartered
1	celery stick, cut in half
3	onions, peeled
12 slices	smoked streaky bacon, diced
1 bunch	flatleaf parsley, chopped
2 tbsp	malt vinegar
16	medium oysters, shucked
	salt and freshly ground black pepper

Pastry

300g	plain flour
1 tsp	salt
150g	cold butter, diced
30g	crème fraiche
1	egg, beaten, to glaze

Place the heads in a large saucepan, cover with cold water and season with a generous pinch of salt. Add the bay leaves, carrot, celery and 1 onion, cut into quarters. Bring the water to the boil, then turn down the heat and simmer the heads for 2 hours or until tender. The meat and the skin should be falling off the bone. Remove the pan from the heat and leave the heads to cool in the liquid.

Meanwhile, make the pastry. Put the flour, salt and butter in a bowl and work everything together with your fingertips until the mixture is the consistency of crumbs. Add the crème fraiche, then slowly add 50ml of cold water and bring the dough together. Do not overwork it. Wrap the dough in cling film and chill it in the fridge for 2 hours.

Remove the heads and pick off all the meat and gelatinous skin from the bones and put it all in a bowl. Pay particular attention to all the cavities and the area below the jaw. Peel and chop the tongues. You should get about 900g of meat.

Strain the stock and keep it for making soups and broths – add pearl barley to make another really delicious meal.

Preheat the oven to 200°C/Fan 180°C/Gas 6. Slice the remaining onions. Gently fry the diced bacon in a pan to render the fat, then add the onions and cook them for 10 minutes until lightly coloured. Add the bacon and onions and the chopped parsley to the meat in the bowl, then season with plenty of pepper and the vinegar.

Pile half the meat mixture into a 1.5 litre pie dish, then add the oysters and top with the rest of the meat. Roll out the pastry and lay it over the pie. Crimp the edges and brush the pastry with the beaten egg. Bake the pie in the preheated oven for 40 minutes and serve hot.

Lamb's Lights Kebabs

Lamb lights are actually the lungs of the animal. They are very nutritious, cheap to buy and good to eat if cooked properly. Their best-known use is in haggis, but in this dish they are the star of the show.

Serves 6 as a starter

500g	lamb's lights, cut into 2cm cubes
	sage leaves
300g	caul fat
	olive oil
	juice of 1 lemon
	salt and freshly ground black pepper

Soak wooden skewers in cold water so they don't burn when you put them on the barbecue. Thread cubes of lamb's lights on to the skewers, alternating them with sage leaves – use 4 leaves per skewer. Season well with salt and pepper.

Wrap each skewer in a piece of caul fat to keep the meat moist. Lights don't have any fat so can easily dry out. Brush the caul fat with olive oil.

Cook the kebabs on a barbecue – not too hot – or under a preheated grill for 15 minutes. Turn them regularly and brush them with oil occasionally.

Once the meat is cooked, remove it from the skewers and sprinkle it with fresh lemon juice. Serve with a crunchy green salad.

SALADES
LEGUMES ET SAUCES

SALADES, LEGUMES ET SAUCES:
salads, vegetables and sauces – accompaniments

The following recipes can be used with any kind of dish but are all favourites of mine to accompany offal. I find the sharpness of chicory and the nutty flavour of celeriac, for example, are both great for offsetting the richness of some liver and kidney dishes. Some carbs are a must for soaking up the meaty juices of a stew or casserole and while boiled potatoes often do the trick, a potato gratin is always welcome.

I like to keep a selection of chutneys and relishes – home-made are best of course – to serve with cold cuts and terrines such as brawns. Their slightly sweet, sharp and spicy taste adds just the right tang to balance the flavours. And I've included a few classic sauces here, such as red wine sauce, which is perfect with the calf's brain and black pudding wellington on page 154, and, of course mayonnaise and tartare sauce.

Good stock is essential for many of the recipes in this book, adding wonderful body and savour to a dish. While you can buy excellent fresh stocks in the supermarket nowadays I have included recipes for a range of stocks should you want to go the extra mile and make your own.

Coleslaw

I serve this with the pork faggots on page 100 but it is also very good with dishes such as brawn (see pages 96–97).

Serves 10

900g	white cabbage
1	onion, peeled and thinly sliced
1	carrot, peeled and grated
1½ tbsp	coarse sea salt
2 tbsp	cider vinegar
1 tbsp	sugar
125ml	mayonnaise
125ml	buttermilk
	ground white pepper

Shred or thinly slice the cabbage and put it in a colander with the onion and the grated carrot. Add the salt and toss well, then leave to drain for a couple of hours. Squeeze out as much moisture as you can with your hands, then pile everything into a large bowl.

Stir the vinegar and sugar together in a jug until the sugar has dissolved. Add the mayonnaise and buttermilk, then season with pepper to taste. Fold this dressing into the cabbage. Taste to check the seasoning and adjust if necessary, then put the salad in the fridge until you're ready to serve.

Salt-baked Celeriac

I love this way of cooking celeriac and it can be served hot as a vegetable or cold in a salad.

Serves 4

1	celeriac (about 500g)
4	bay leaves, chopped
1 sprig	rosemary, chopped
100g	plain flour, plus extra for dusting
1 tbsp	cracked black pepper
4	egg whites
100g	fine table salt
300g	rock salt
	zest of 1 lemon

Preheat the oven to 200°C/Fan 180°C/Gas 6. Scrub the celeriac until it's thoroughly clean. No need to peel it.

Mix the herbs with the rest of the ingredients to make a paste. Roll it out on a floured surface to about 1cm thick and wrap it round the celeriac to encase the vegetable completely. Make sure there are no gaps.

Place the celeriac on a baking tray and bake it in the preheated oven for 1½ hours. Remove it and leave to cool for 10 minutes before cracking open the salt crust. Peel off the salty crust and skin, slice the celeriac and serve it with a knob of butter.

Pomme Darphin au Brie

A pomme darphin is like a beautiful big potato cake made with grated potato. This version is stuffed with slices of brie to make it even more delicious.

Serves 4

4	large potatoes, peeled and coarsely grated
2	shallots, peeled and thinly sliced
2 tbsp	roughly chopped parsley
2 tbsp	duck fat
4	5mm slices of brie
	salt and freshly ground black pepper

Put the grated potato in a bowl and add the shallots and parsley. Mix well, then squeeze out as much of the excess water as you can with your hands.

Preheat the oven to 200°C/Fan 180°C/Gas 6. Heat the duck fat in an ovenproof frying pan – one with a 20cm diameter is perfect. Add half the potato mix and press it down with a fork to level the surface. Place the slices of brie on top, followed by the rest of the potato mixture. Press it down well around the edges and on top.

Cook over a medium heat for 10 minutes, then carefully slide the darphin out on to a plate, flip it and slide it back into the pan to cook on the other side for a further 10 minutes. Then transfer the pan to the oven and cook for 15 minutes. Leave it to cool for a few minutes before cutting and serving.

Celeriac and Potato Gratin

This gratin is quick and easy to make and goes beautifully with stews and casseroles.

Serves 6–8

1	celeriac
2	large potatoes
1 litre	whole milk
2	garlic cloves, crushed
2	bay leaves
	grating of nutmeg
250ml	double cream
	salt and freshly ground black pepper

Peel the celeriac and cut it into quarters. Using a mandolin or a very sharp knife, cut the celeriac into fine slices – about 2mm is ideal. Peel the potatoes and cut them into 2mm slices.

Preheat the oven to 200°C/180°C/Gas 6. Pour the milk into a large saucepan, add the garlic, bay leaves and nutmeg and season with salt and pepper. Bring the milk to the boil, then add the cream and the sliced celeriac and potatoes. Cook for 5 minutes, then remove the pan from the heat.

Pour everything into a baking dish and level the surface. Cover the dish with foil and bake for 20 minutes. Remove the foil and bake for another 20 minutes.

Chicory Salad with Walnuts and Golden Raisins

Chicory, also known as endive or Belgian endive, is available in red or white varieties and has a good crunchy texture. The flavour marries well with walnuts and raisins to make this excellent salad.

Serves 4

2	red chicory
2	white chicory
60g	golden raisins
60g	walnut halves, roughly chopped
1	spring onion, finely sliced
4 tbsp	walnut oil
2 tbsp	red wine vinegar
1 tsp	wholegrain mustard
	salt and freshly ground black pepper

Separate the heads of chicory into leaves and put them in a bowl. Blanch the raisins for 5 minutes in a pan of boiling water, then drain and add them to the chicory together with the walnuts and spring onion.

Whisk the oil, vinegar, mustard, salt and pepper to make the dressing. Just before serving, add the dressing to the salad and toss well.

Roast Beetroot

This is a really simple side dish, which goes well with pork dishes.
Use different coloured beetroots if you can find them.

Serves 6

6–8	medium beetroots
2 sprigs	rosemary, roughly chopped
6	bay leaves
	olive oil
	coarse sea salt

Preheat the oven to 200°C/Fan 180°C/Gas 6. Wash the beetroots and place them on a large piece of foil. Sprinkle the rosemary and bay leaves on top, then wrap the beetroots in the foil, sealing the edges to make a parcel. Bake them in the oven until tender – this will take about an hour.

Remove the beetroots from the oven and open the parcel. Once the beetroots are cool the skin will come off easily. Cut the beetroots into slices and sprinkle them with a drizzle of olive oil and some coarse sea salt.

Green Tomato Relish

This is an excellent accompaniment for terrines or cold cuts such as black pudding with chestnuts (see pages 84–85).

Makes 2 small jars

600g	green tomatoes
1	shallot, chopped
80g	demerara sugar
60ml	white wine vinegar
1 tsp	ground cumin
2 tsp	salt
2	green chillies
3 tbsp	chopped coriander

Bring a saucepan of water to the boil, add the tomatoes and blanch them for a few seconds. Refresh them in iced water, then peel and deseed them. Roughly chop the flesh.

Put the shallot in a saucepan with the sugar, vinegar, cumin, salt and 60ml of water. Simmer until the shallot is cooked and the pan is almost dry. Chop the chillies and add them to the pan, including the seeds if you want the relish to be very spicy, then add the chopped tomatoes. Cover the pan and simmer for 10 minutes.

Add the chopped coriander, mix well and bring to the boil. Tip the relish into a food processor and blend until smooth. Spoon it into a sterilised jar and leave to cool. This keeps well in the fridge for about a week.

Beetroot Ketchup

I serve this with the bone marrow croquettes on page 132, but it is also great served with grilled meat.

Makes 1 large jar

1 tsp	sunflower oil
1	red onion, peeled and chopped
60g	button mushrooms, chopped
50g	demerara sugar
2 tsp	sea salt
1 tsp	chilli powder
2 tsp	smoked paprika
1 tsp	ground coriander
1 tsp	ground cumin
160ml	cider vinegar
400g	cooked, peeled beetroots

Warm the oil in a saucepan and add the onion and mushrooms. Sweat them until they are tender and any liquid has evaporated.

Add the sugar, salt and spices, continue to cook for 2–3 minutes, then add the vinegar and beetroots. Simmer for 10 minutes, then tip everything into a food processor and blitz until smooth.

Pour the ketchup into a sterilised jar and leave it cool. You can then store it in the fridge for up to a couple of weeks.

Red Onion Chutney

This is the perfect chutney to serve with chicken liver parfait
(see pages 38–39).

Makes 2 jars

1kg	red onion, thinly sliced
½ tsp	crushed black peppercorns
8g	fresh root ginger, grated
1 pinch	ground cloves
1	red chilli, finely chopped
250g	dark soft brown sugar
600ml	white wine vinegar
250g	tomatoes, peeled, deseeded and diced
100g	sultanas
	salt

Put all the ingredients, except the diced tomatoes, sultanas and salt, into a wide saucepan. Place the pan over a medium heat and cook, stirring occasionally, until the onions are soft and the mixture is thick and syrupy. This will take about 25 minutes.

Add the tomatoes and sultanas, season with salt and stir well, then cook for another 10 minutes. Check the seasoning, then pour the chutney into sterilised jars and seal while hot. Leave to cool, then store in the fridge.

Mayonnaise

A good home-made mayonnaise is an ideal accompaniment for cold cuts and terrines. Add chopped fresh herbs such as chives, tarragon, parsley or dill for a herb mayonnaise.

Makes about 600ml

2	free-range egg yolks
1 tbsp	Dijon mustard
1 tsp	fine salt
½ tbsp	white wine vinegar
500ml	vegetable oil
50ml	extra virgin olive oil

Put the egg yolks, mustard, salt and vinegar in a round-bottomed bowl and mix with a balloon whisk until smooth. Gradually pour in the oils in a steady stream, whisking constantly until the mixture is rich and creamy.

Store the mayonnaise in a covered container in the fridge. It keeps well for up to a week.

Beurre Blanc

This is one of the classic sauces in French cuisine. It's generally served with fish and I like it with the terrine of sweetbreads and lobster on pages 150–152.

Makes about 300ml

100ml	dry white wine
1 tbsp	white wine vinegar
2	shallots, peeled and finely chopped
50ml	double cream
200g	cold unsalted butter, cubed
	salt and freshly ground black pepper

Put the wine, vinegar and shallots in a thick-based saucepan. Bring to the boil and continue to cook until the liquid is reduced by half. Add the cream and boil for another minute, then lower the heat and gradually whisk in the cubes of cold butter.

You can keep the shallots in the sauce if you like, but for a smoother finish, pass the sauce through a fine sieve. Season with salt and pepper to taste.

Garlic Croutons

Bread should never go to waste and you can make these crunchy croutons with any kind of bread as well as baguette. Croutons are a great way of adding texture and flavour to a salad.

Makes enough for 10

1	day-old baguette
1 tbsp	olive oil
2	garlic cloves, bruised
	salt and freshly ground black pepper

Thinly slice the baguette. Heat the olive oil in a wide frying pan over a medium heat, add the garlic cloves and cook until they release their aroma. Add the slices of baguette, in batches, and fry them gently until golden brown. Drain the croutons on kitchen paper and season with salt and pepper.

For small fried croutons, cut some white bread into 5mm cubes or tear it into pieces for a more rustic garnish. Heat enough vegetable oil in a pan to shallow fry the bread. When it is hot and smoking, add the bread with a couple of cloves of bruised garlic and a sprig of thyme. Cook until golden, then drain and season lightly with salt.

Tartare Sauce

A classic sauce, with a good punchy flavour, this is just right with the beef tendon meatballs on pages 194–195.

Serves 6

2	egg yolks
2 tsp	Dijon mustard
2 tbsp	red wine vinegar
250ml	vegetable oil
1	small shallot, peeled and chopped
2 tbsp	chopped chervil, tarragon, parsley
1 tsp	fine capers (optional)
1 tsp	chopped gherkins (optional)
	salt and freshly ground black pepper

Put the egg yolks in a bowl, then whisk in the mustard and red wine vinegar and season with salt and pepper. Slowly add the oil, a little at a time, whisking constantly. Finally mix in the chopped shallot, herbs and the capers and gherkins, if using.

Red Wine Sauce

Another classic sauce, this is traditionally served with steak but it's also good with the calf's brain and black pudding wellington on pages 154–155.

Makes 700ml

120g	beef trimmings (bone or sinew)
	olive oil
1 bottle	full-bodied red wine (Syrah or Shiraz)
100ml	port
1	onion, peeled and sliced
2	shallots, peeled and sliced
80g	smoked bacon, chopped
1 tsp	cracked white and black peppercorns
2 litres	veal stock

Fry the beef trimmings in a pan with a little olive oil until crisp. Drain off the fat, add the wine and port and reduce by half, occasionally skimming off the fat and scum that come to the surface.

Heat a little olive oil in another pan and cook the onion, shallots and bacon until well browned. Add the peppercorns and then pour in the reduced wine, followed by the stock. Bring to the boil and skim, then turn down the heat and simmer for 35 minutes. Pass the sauce through a fine sieve.

To serve, bring the sauce to the boil and reduce until slightly thickened. Take the pan off the heat and whisk in some cold butter, cut into small cubes.

Chicken Stock

Makes about 4 litres

2kg	chicken bones or wing tips
1	calf's foot, split
1	onion, peeled and roughly chopped
1	small leek, roughly chopped
2	celery sticks, roughly chopped
2 sprigs	thyme
6	parsley stalks

Place the bones, or wing tips, and the calf's foot in a large saucepan, cover with 5 litres of water and bring to the boil. Skim off the scum and fat that comes to the surface. Turn the heat down, add the remaining ingredients and simmer for 1½ hours, skimming occasionally.

Pass the stock through a fine sieve and leave to cool. It can be kept in the fridge for up to 5 days or it can be frozen.

Fish Stock

Makes about 2 litres

1kg	bones and heads from white fish
	(sole, whiting, turbot)
4 tbsp	unsalted butter
1	small onion, peeled and roughly chopped
1	celery stick, roughly chopped
60g	dry white wine
6	parsley stalks
1	bay leaf

Remove any gills from the fish heads, then soak the heads and bones in cold water for 3–4 hours. Remove them from the water and chop them roughly.

Melt the butter in a deep saucepan and sweat the onion and celery over a low heat until softened. Add the fish bones and heads and cook for 2–3 minutes, stirring frequently.

Pour in the wine, turn up the heat and reduce by half. Add 2 litres of water and the herbs, then bring to the boil, skimming frequently. Lower the heat and simmer, uncovered, for 25 minutes. Pass the stock through a muslin-lined sieve and leave to cool. It can be kept in the fridge for 2–3 days or it can be frozen.

Vegetable Stock

Makes 2 litres

1	carrot
2	shallots
1	small onion
2	celery sticks
1	leek (green top part only)
1	bay leaf
2 sprigs	thyme
	handful of parsley stalks

Peel or trim and roughly chop all the vegetables and put them in a large saucepan with 2½ litres of water. Add the herbs and bring the water to the boil. Simmer for about 35 minutes, then strain the stock before using. It can be kept in the fridge for up to 5 days.

Veal Stock

Makes about 3.5 litres

1.5kg	veal knuckle bones, chopped
1	calf's foot, split
	olive oil
1	large onion, peeled and roughly chopped
2	large carrots, peeled and roughly chopped
1	celery stick, roughly chopped
2	garlic cloves, peeled
2 sprigs	thyme
½ tbsp	tomato purée

Preheat the oven to 220°C/Fan 200°C/Gas 7. Put the bones and calf's foot in a roasting pan with a little oil and roast them in the oven, turning them occasionally until they're brown all over. Transfer them to a large saucepan.

Put the onion, carrots and celery into the roasting pan and roast them in the oven until golden, turning them frequently with a wooden spatula. Pour off any excess fat and put the vegetables into the saucepan with the bones. Place the roasting pan over a high heat and add 500ml of water. Bring to the boil, scraping the bottom of the pan to loosen any caramelised bits, then pour everything into the saucepan with the bones.

Add the remaining ingredients and another 4½ litres of water and bring to the boil. Skim off the scum and fat, then turn down the heat and simmer gently for 3½ hours, skimming occasionally. Pass the stock through a fine sieve and leave to cool. The stock can be kept in the fridge for up to 7 days or it can be frozen.

Beef Stock or Broth

Marrowbones, knuckles, ribs or oxtail tips with little or no meat on them are all fine for this stock. Ask your butcher to chop the bones up for you. You can use this recipe for the broth to go with the leberknodel on page 204.

Makes about 4 litres

2kg	beef bones, chopped
2	carrots
1	onion
1	leek
2	celery stalks
	olive oil
4	garlic cloves, chopped
2	bay leaves
500ml	white wine
1 tbsp	black peppercorns

Preheat the oven to 220°C/Fan 200°C/Gas 7. Put the bones in a large roasting tin. Peel and wash the vegetables and chop them roughly, then drizzle them with a little oil and add them to the bones. Add the chopped garlic and the bay leaves. Roast for about 30 minutes until the bones and vegetables are browned and caramelised, turning them a couple of times.

Transfer everything to a deep stock pan or large saucepan, discarding any fat in the roasting tin. Put the tin on the hob and add the wine. Deglaze, scraping up any sticky bits from the bottom of the tin, then add this to the bones in the pan.

Add cold water to the pan to cover everything by at least 20cm. Bring to the boil, then turn the heat down to a very gentle simmer. Skim well and cook for at least 6 hours. You may need to top up the liquid with a little hot water from time to time to ensure the bones stay covered.

Leave to cool, then skim off any fat and pass the stock through a fine sieve. Use immediately or chill for later use. This stock freezes well.

CONVERSIONS

We have used metric measurements throughout this book, but the following tables give imperial equivalents should you need them. When following a recipe, always stick to the same system and never use a mixture of imperial and metric. Some measurements have been rounded up or down for simplicity's sake.

OVEN TEMPERATURES

°C	Fan oven °C	°F	Gas
110	90	225	¼
120	100	250	½
140	120	275	1
150	130	300	2
160	140	325	3
180	160	350	4
190	170	375	5
200	180	400	6
220	200	425	7
230	210	450	8
240	220	475	9

WEIGHT

Metric (grams and kilograms)	Imperial (ounces and pounds)
25g	1oz
50g	2oz
75g	3oz
100g	4oz
150g	5oz
175g	6oz
200g	7oz
225g	8oz
250g	9oz
275g	10oz
350g	12oz
375g	13oz
400g	14oz
450g	1lb
550g	1lb 3oz
675g	1lb 8oz
750g	1lb 10oz
900g	2lb
1kg	2lb and 3oz
1.5kg	3lb

VOLUME

Metric (millilitres and litres)	Imperial (UK fluid ounces and pints)
25ml	1fl oz
50ml	2fl oz
85ml	3fl oz
100ml	3½ fl oz
125ml	4fl oz
150ml	5fl oz
175ml	6fl oz
200ml	7fl oz
225ml	8fl oz
275ml	9fl oz
300ml	10½fl oz
450ml	16fl oz
600ml	20fl oz (1 pint)
700ml	1¼ pints
900ml	1½ pints
1 litre	1¾ pints
1.2 litres	2 pints
1.75 litres	3 pints
2.25 litres	4 pints
2.75 litres	5 pints

LENGTH

Metric (centimetres)	Imperial (inches)
1cm	½in
2.5cm	1in
5cm	2in
7.5cm	3in
10cm	4in
15cm	6in
20cm	8in
25cm	10in
30cm	12in
50cm	20in

EQUIPMENT

You don't need lots of expensive equipment for making the recipes in this book, but one thing I would recommend is a mincing machine. Some food mixers do have mincer attachments, but I think the old-fashioned, hand-cranked sort that clamp to the side of the table do a great job. They are cheap, efficient and there's less chance of mincing your fingers!

If you're planning on boiling pigs' heads you will need an extra large pan, and for making terrines, a terrine dish with a lid is useful. I prefer the ceramic ones to the silicone versions. You can also make terrines in a loaf tin.

The only other thing to add is get to know your butcher. A friendly butcher who will order unusual items for you, bone heads and split trotters will be a great help.

INDEX

My thanks to

Chef Rachel for testing and helping with the research, Jinny Johnson for her patience and foodie enthusiasm, Edwina Simon for making sense of my scribbles, Amanda Harris and Lucie Stericker at Orion for their support and creativity, and my agent Andrew Nurnberg.

I'd also like to thank the Fort family for their appetite!